WRITINGS OF JOHN BAILLIE

The Roots of Religion in the Human Soul
The Interpretation of Religion
The Place of Jesus Christ in Modern Christianity
And the Life Everlasting
A Diary of Private Prayer
Our Knowledge of God
Invitation to Pilgrimage
The Prospects of Spiritual Renewal
What is Christian Civilization?
The Mind of the Modern University
Spiritual Religion
The Belief in Progress
The Human Situation
Natural Science and the Spiritual Life
A Diary of Readings
The Idea of Revelation in Recent Thought
The Sense of the Presence of God
Christian Devotion
A Reasoned Faith
Baptism and Conversion

BAPTISM
and
CONVERSION

JOHN BAILLIE

BAPTISM
and
CONVERSION

CHARLES SCRIBNER'S SONS
NEW YORK

Copyright © 1963 F. Jewel Baillie

All rights reserved. No part of this book
may be reproduced in any form without
the permission of Charles Scribner's Sons.

A-9.63[V]

Printed in the United States of America
Library of Congress Catalog Card Number 63-17936

FOREWORD

A number of those present at the delivery of these lectures have recently been pressing for their publication. Therefore, at a time when much thought, study and lively discussion are being directed to the subject of Baptism—particularly by the Church of Scotland and the World Council of Churches—it seems an appropriate moment at which to add a small contribution from my late husband's pen.

In 1955 these lectures were delivered as the Carnahan Lectures at the Facultad Evangélica de Teologia in Buenos Aires, and later the same Faculty arranged for their translation into Spanish, and for their publication the following year.

The lectures were also given in whole or in part as the Birks Lectures in the Faculty of Divinity of McGill University, Montreal; as the Reinecker Lectures in Virginia Theological Seminary, Alexandria, Virginia, U.S.A.; and also as the Auburn Extension Lectures in Union Theological Seminary, New York City. I am most grateful to the authorities of all these Colleges for agreeing so heartily to their publication in English, and for encouraging me to take this step.

Foreword

Further, I would like to thank Dr. James Brown for initially reading through the MS, and for his ready help and suggestions, as also Professor John McIntyre, and Professor W. R. Forrester—the latter most kindly reading proofs and giving constant advice.

Edinburgh, 1963   F. Jewel Baillie

CONTENTS

FOREWORD   7

I. BAPTISM AND REGENERATION   11

1. *The Problem*
2. *Baptism in the New Testament*
3. *The Roman Teaching*
4. *The Lutheran Teaching*
5. *The Teaching of Calvin*
6. *The Teaching of the Reformed Churches*
7. *The Teaching of the Baptist Churches*
8. *An Attempted Conclusion*

II. PRE-CHRISTIAN CONVERSION   49

9. *Conversion to a Religion and Conversion within a Religion*
10. *Conversion within the Pagan Religions*
11. *Conversion in the Old Testament*
12. *Conversion to a Faith following on Conversion within another Faith*

Contents

III. THE TEACHING OF THE CHRISTIAN CHURCHES ABOUT CONVERSION   65

13. *The Medieval and Roman Teaching*
14. *The Lutheran Teaching*
15. *The Reformed Teaching*
16. *The Influence of the Later Evangelical Movements*

IV. THE NATURE OF THE CONVERSION EXPERIENCE   89

17. *"Evangelical" Conversion Analyzed*
18. *Psychological "Readjustment"*
19. *The Relation of such Readjustment to the Christian Gospel*
20. *Is a "Conversion Experience" Necessary?*

INDEX   113

I

Baptism and Regeneration

1

The Problem

WHAT I propose to do is to elucidate certain important divergences of theological opinion which manifested themselves within the Commission on Evangelism which was set up in preparation for the Evanston Assembly of the World Council of Churches, and at the same time to indicate the position to which I myself have been led. And I can make no better beginning than by quoting part of a statement made by Bishop Stephen Neill at the first meeting of that Commission in Wadham College, Oxford. The Bishop began by saying that "the moment we go beyond vague generalisation, it becomes apparent that there are within the Church widely different ideas as to what evangelism is, and as to how it ought to be carried out," and further that "at no point is this disagreement more apparent than on the question of conversion," so that "even the meeting of minds in rational discussion of the problem is not easy to achieve." He then proceeded as follows:

> It may help to clarify the issue, if we state in the extremest form two antithetic approaches to

Baptism and Conversion

the problem, recognizing that there is an element of exaggeration in the statements, and that each is open to criticism on various grounds:

(a) Conversion is the beginning of real Christian life. Christian nurture, education and worship may be valuable preparations. But no one is, or should be called a Christian until he has personally encountered God in Jesus Christ, until he has personally repented, until he has personally accepted God's gift of salvation through faith in Christ, until by his faith he has individually been born again. The reality of the Church in the world depends on there being enough people who have passed through this experience, and through whom it can be passed on to others.

(b) Christian life begins at baptism, when by the grace of God operating through the Church, original sin is taken away, and the divine life is sown as a seed in the heart of man. Through Christian teaching, through life in the Church and through the grace of the sacraments, this seed can grow. Though growth may be hindered by resistance on the part of the individual, nevertheless it is a continuous process. To demand any other decisive new beginning is to deny the reality of the grace of God. What the individual is called to do is to recognize the reality of what God has already done in him and to take that seriously.

In general, this second position, with considerable variations, is that maintained by the Roman Catholic and Orthodox Churches, and by the state Churches of Europe, where it is taken for granted that the normal sequence of Christian

Baptism and Regeneration

nurture, worship, special religious instruction and Confirmation will lead on to full membership and responsibility in the Church. The first position, again with many variations, is that maintained by the evangelical Free Churches, and by evangelical movements within the more traditional Churches. In the one case membership in the Church is expected to lead on to personal Christian experience. In the other, personal Christian experience is regarded as the pre-condition for effective membership in the Church.

It may be, as Bishop Neill allows, that neither position would usually be stated in a form quite so antithetic to the other as that in which it here appears, yet there is no doubt that we have here to do with a radical divergence of outlook such as, in the Bishop's own words, "has proved in many places an insuperable obstacle to common planning and action" [1] in the sphere of evangelism. What I shall attempt to do is to investigate more closely the real nature of this divergence, to enquire into its causes and, if possible, to move a little way towards the resolution of it.

[1] All citations in this chapter are taken from the *Scottish Journal of Theology*, Vol. 3, 1950, pp. 352 and 353.

2

Baptism in the New Testament

It seems certain that we have here to do, not with a single issue, but with a complication of several different issues, albeit there is something of a natural connection between them all. In attempting to disentangle these, I shall begin by asking what we are to believe about baptism. I shall not, however, deal by any means with all the questions that may be raised about baptism, but shall confine myself, as far as may be, to the question of its relation to those other terms mentioned in the Bishop's statement—conversion, the new birth, and the beginning of the Christian life. And I shall proceed by setting out as clearly as I am able the main views that have been held concerning this relation in the course of Christian history.

The view taken by the New Testament itself is, of course, still very debatable ground, since every one of the later views claims to find its support there. We cannot then afford to be dogmatic about the New Testament teaching, but there are one or two things that may surely be said without fear of contradiction. The first is that in the New Testament baptism always marks the incorporation of the individual within the Body of Christ. "By

Baptism and Regeneration

one Spirit were we all baptized into one body."[1] It is essentially a rite of purification, marking the washing away of sin, and in at least one passage—where we read of the man who "has forgotten that he was purged from his old sins"[2]—the specific reference is to sins committed before baptism. Further, it seems clear that, as marking incorporation into the Body of Christ, baptism is inseparably connected with regeneration or being born again. In the Epistle to Titus it is spoken of as the *loutron paliggenesias* which we may translate either as the washing of regeneration or the bath of rebirth.[3] St. Paul also writes to the Corinthians, "You were washed, you were made holy, you were justified, in the name of our Lord Jesus Christ, and in the Spirit of the Lord."[4] I make no pronouncement here about the question which has been the object of so much controversy, namely, the precise nature of the connection in the mind of the New Testament writers between the outward rite and the inward renewal; I say only that they are inseparably connected, and should always go together. Baptists will here agree with paedobaptists, and indeed it is precisely on this ground that the former reject the practice of infant baptism, because they cannot see how infants can be regenerated.

[1] I Cor. xii, 13.
[2] II Peter i, 9.
[3] Titus iii, 5.
[4] I Cor. vi, 11.

3

The Roman Teaching

HAVING said this about the New Testament, let us now turn to the teaching of the pre-Reformation Church in the West or—what is for our purpose very nearly the same thing—to the Roman teaching as it is to this day. And let us ask how, according to Roman teaching, a man becomes a Christian. The answer given is different in the case of an adult and in the case of an infant. In the former case a man becomes a Christian when he is enabled by God to have faith and on the basis of that faith receives baptism. Such faith, according to *The Catholic Encyclopaedia*, "is an act of the understanding, whereby we firmly hold as true what God has revealed"; yet though "it is itself an act of the understanding, it requires the influence of the will which moves the intellect to assent." It is said to proceed by steps.

> The first step . . . is the investigation and examination of the credentials of the Church, which often is a painful labour lasting for years. . . . The intellectual conviction, however, is not yet the act of faith. One may hesitate or refuse to take the next step, which is 'the good will to

Baptism and Regeneration

believe. . . .' This leads to the final act, the act of faith itself: I believe what the Church teaches, because God has revealed it.[1]

We note that here faith means assent to doctrine, a holding for true of certain propositions; though it does not mean merely *seeing* that they are true but *accepting* them as such—so that the will is involved.

Within Christian civilization, however, the normal case is that of admission into the Church in infancy. All infants should be baptized, and

> the effect of this sacrament is the remission of all sin, original and actual; likewise of all punishment which is due to sin. As a consequence, no satisfaction for past sins is enjoined upon those who are baptized; and if they die before they commit any sin, they attain immediately to the kingdom of heaven and the vision of God.[2]

Baptism should then be followed, according to Roman teaching, by the further sacrament of confirmation, "in which the Holy Ghost is given to those already baptized, in order to make them strong and perfect Christians." [3] In baptism sins are remitted; in confirmation the Holy Spirit is conferred—by anointing with oil and the laying on of the bishop's hands. It may be remarked in passing that it

[1] *The Catholic Encyclopaedia*: article on "Conversion."
[2] *The Catholic Encyclopaedia*: article on "Baptism."
[3] *The Catholic Encyclopaedia*: article on "Conversion."

Baptism and Conversion

is more than doubtful whether there is any New Testament ground for such a distinction. The question has been well argued by Bultmann in his *Theology of the New Testament* [4] and by Cullmann in his little book on *Baptism in the New Testament*,[5] but both conclude that in the New Testament the Spirit is conferred in baptism, and that here precisely lies the specific difference of Christian from Johannine baptism.

To continue then with the Roman teaching, the Catechism of the Council of Trent says that infants may be confirmed at baptism, i.e., immediately following on the baptismal ceremony, as in the practice in Spain and in the Eastern Orthodox Church, but that is not expedient before the use of reason and is most fitting after the age of seven years has been reached. Confirmation is not absolutely necessary to salvation, but it is wrong to neglect it, and its reception is ordinarily obligatory. Protestants of what is called the evangelical tradition will perhaps now wish to ask: Are those baptized in infancy, and confirmed either then or at the age of seven, expected to undergo any later decisive change or experience such as might be called conversion? The answer is that nothing further is required for salvation unless after baptism they commit mortal sin. If mortal sin is committed, then a further sacrament is required, namely, *poenitentia*. This Latin word may be translated into English as either penitence

---

[4] Vol. I, English translation, pp. 138f.
[5] English translation, pp. 11f.

Baptism and Regeneration

or penance, and to English-speaking Protestants the two words suggest different meanings. But in Latin, and in most other languages, as in the German word *Busse*, there is only the one concept covering the two English words. All mortal sins must be confessed and the sacrament of penance received for them. "It is useful to confess also venial sins," [6] but this is not necessary, nor is the administration of *poenitentia* required for them, the grace given at baptism being sufficient for their remission. Sometimes the word conversion is used for each act of repentance after mortal sin, but of course such conversions do not coincide with a person's first becoming a Christian.

[6] Cardinal Gasparri's *Catechism for Little Children*, Q. 20.

4

The Lutheran Teaching

LET us next ask: What change in this teaching did the Reformation bring with it? The answer to this question is very complicated. The Roman teaching, however defective we may regard it, is clear and precise and everywhere the same. The Protestant teaching, on the other hand, though grappling with the realities of the situation on what we must think to be a deeper level, not only varies considerably from one Reformer to another, but is seldom set forth with the same precision. Let us take Luther first.

Luther held fast to the Catholic doctrine of baptismal regeneration. In his *Small Catechism* of 1529 the question "What happens at baptism?" is answered by saying that "It worketh forgiveness of sins, delivers from death and the devil, and gives everlasting salvation to all that believe it." Nor did he for a moment break with the Catholic teaching that the infants of Christian parents should be baptized. When he discusses baptism, it is nearly always infant baptism that he has in mind. To him adult baptism would be a rare occurrence, since all the people he knew—except the occasional wandering Jew—

Baptism and Regeneration

would have been baptized in infancy, and no more than the other Reformers did he give much thought to the evangelization of the pagan world. To Luther, then, regeneration normally took place in infancy. Yet here was a difficulty. The Roman teaching had been that faith is required as a precondition of the baptism of adults, but not in the case of infants. But what then of Luther's fundamental principle of salvation by faith alone? Well, he seems to have wavered in his answer. His first answer was that the faith required in this instance is the *fides aliena* of the Church, or of the parents and sponsors, but he finally came to prefer the alternative idea of a *fides infantilis*, an inchoate yet real faith already present in the souls of babies at baptism. Incidentally, we may note that both these answers are rejected by Karl Barth in his well-known brochure on *The Doctrine of Baptism*, and also by Emil Brunner in his book translated into English under the title *The Divine-Human Encounter*. Both add that any such idea cries out for complementation by a further sacrament of confirmation after years of discretion are reached, in which the missing element of personal response is supplied; but both deny (as indeed we have found the New Testament scholars Bultmann and Cullmann also doing) that there is any scriptural warrant for this kind of separation between baptism and confirmation. Hence Barth seems to break with the tradition of infant baptism altogether, and Brunner to be on the point of doing so.

Baptism and Conversion

Barth and Brunner, however, are not Lutherans but Calvinists; and meanwhile we must note that all the Lutheran formularies follow Luther in holding that regeneration takes place at baptism. In the Augsburg Confession (1530) it is taught that baptism

> is necessary to salvation, and that by baptism the grace of God is offered, and that children are to be baptized who, by baptism being oblates to God, are received into God's favour.[1]

In the later *Formula of Concord* (1576–1584) it is said that baptism effects regeneration or renovation (*renovatio, Erneuerung*), and that at baptism infants are accordingly "born again." On the other hand, we must note that these Lutheran documents speak also of regeneration as something which is not *completed* in a moment, but only in later life; and as we proceed we shall find something of the same sort being said by the Calvinists. Sometimes also Luther seems to distinguish between regeneration, which takes place at baptism, and justification, which comes later;[2] but he does so only waveringly, and I doubt whether it was of great importance for his thought.

At all events, the most important respect in which Luther broke with the Roman teaching was the following. I have said that according to Roman doctrine baptism

[1] Article IX.
[2] Cf. *The Encyclopaedia of Religion and Ethics:* article on "Baptism," in Vol. II.

Baptism and Regeneration

conveys remission only of original sin and of actual sins committed before baptism—perhaps also of venial sins committed thereafter; so that an entirely fresh bestowal of forgiveness and grace is required on the occasion of each later absolution from mortal sin after due penance. But Luther taught that baptism is efficacious for the remission of *all* sin, so that afterwards it is sufficient to "remember one's baptism" and to trust in the assurance of forgiveness then once for all conveyed.[3] On this he lays the greatest stress; nothing is more characteristic of him; and it has often been remarked that on looking back over his past life, and on occasions when later evangelicals would say *Conversus sum*, "I have been converted," Luther rather exclaims *Baptizatus sum*, "I have been baptized." I quote, for instance, the following from Frederick Denison Maurice:

> This at least is certain . . . that the doctrine of Baptismal Regeneration was held by Luther not *in conjunction with* that of Justification by Faith . . . but that he *grounded the one on the other*. 'Believe the warrant of your baptism. You are grafted into Christ; claim your position. You have the Spirit, you are children of God; do not live as if you belonged to the devil.' This was his invariable language, with this he shook the Seven Hills.[4]

[3] Cf. *The Encyclopaedia of Religion and Ethics*, Vol. II, pp. 401b–402a.
[4] *The Kingdom of Christ*, Vol. I, Part II, Chapter IV, p. 323.

5

The Teaching of Calvin

LET us pass now from Lutheranism to Calvinism. Here a certain interest attaches to the Saxon Visitation Articles of 1592, which were prepared by a group of Lutheran divines in opposition to the Crypto-Calvinism already at that date manifesting itself among the Lutherans in the Electorate of Saxony. Here it is taught that

> By baptism, as a bath of rebirth and renewal by the Holy Spirit, God saves us, and works in us such righteousness and purification from our sins that he who perseveres to the end in that covenant and hope does not perish but has eternal life.

While among "the false and erroneous doctrines of the Calvinists," which are to be repudiated, are the opinions

> that baptism does not work and confer regeneration, faith, the grace of God and salvation, but only signifies and seals them; that not all who are baptized in water, but the elect only, attain by it the grace of Christ and the gifts of faith; that regeneration does not take place in and with baptism, but afterwards, at a more advanced age—

Baptism and Regeneration

> yea, and with many not before old age; that salvation does not depend on baptism . . . so that, when the ordinary minister is wanting, the infant should be permitted to die without baptism . . . ; that those who are not elect are necessarily damned, and cannot arrive at salvation though they be baptized *tausendmal* and receive the Eucharist every day, and lead as blameless a life as ever can be led.

It must not, of course, be lightly assumed that these and all the other opinions repudiated in the Articles correctly represent the Calvinist position, but they are, I think, very significant as showing how the difference between Lutheran and Calvinist teaching was regarded in that day and place.

What was Calvin's own view? There are in his *Institutes* two successive chapters, the first "On Baptism" and the second "On Infant Baptism." The former opens in a manner quite reminiscent of Luther by controverting the Roman view that the regeneration accomplished in us at baptism avails only for the remission of past sins, so that for sins committed after baptism a further sacrament of *poenitentia* is required. The truth, he writes, is that

> at whatever time we are baptized, we are washed and purified once for the whole of life. Wherefore, as often as we fall, we must call up the remembrance of our baptism, so as to feel certain and secure of the remission of our sins.

Baptism and Conversion

Baptism, he goes on to say, is itself a sacrament of penance; hence if penance is recommended to us throughout the whole of life, the remembrance of baptism should have the same effect.[1] Yet in this equation of baptism and *poenitentia* he goes further than Luther. To Luther *poenitentia*, though similarly associated with the remembrance of baptism, was something separate and later, being connected, as in the Roman Church, with confession and absolution. But to auricular confession and private absolution Calvin will not give the same place. Hence he even equates *poenitentia* with regeneration. "In one word," he writes, "I interpret *poenitentia* as *regeneratio*." Yet he goes on to say, just as we have already found the Lutherans saying, that, though begun in baptism, regeneration "is not completed in a moment, in a day, or a year, but by continuous, sometimes even by slow, progress."[2]

In the next chapter, "On Paedobaptism," Calvin faces the question how babies can be regenerated, seeing they do not yet possess knowledge of good and evil. The question may well seem more urgent for Calvin than for Luther himself, in view of his above-mentioned identification of baptismal regeneration with *poenitentia*. It has often been remarked that Luther and the Lutherans treat infant baptism as the norm and adult baptism more by way of an exception, whereas Calvin and the Reformed theologians rather think out their doctrines of regeneration in terms of men and women coming to Christ by con-

[1] Book IV, Chapter XV.
[2] Book III, Chapter III, 9.

Baptism and Regeneration

scious decision in maturity and then try to fit infant baptism into that scheme. Most certainly this is what Calvin himself does. And his way of fitting in infant baptism is as follows. Regeneration, he says, may take place in infancy.

> Infants who are to be saved (and that some are saved at this age is certain) must, without question, be previously regenerated by the Lord. . . . the age of infancy is not incapable of receiving sanctification.[3]

But can babies then have faith, or are they regenerated without faith? It appears that Calvin was at first inclined to follow Luther's later idea of a *fides infantilis*—as appears in the first edition of the *Institutes*.[4] But later on he was more hesitant:

> I would not rashly affirm that they [infants] are endued with the same faith which we experience in ourselves, or have any kind of knowledge resembling faith—a question which I prefer to leave in suspense.

What we must rather assert is that

> children are baptised for future repentance and faith. Though these are not yet formed in them,

[3] Book IV, Chapter XVI, 17, 18.
[4] Cf. R. S. Wallace, *Calvin's Doctrine of the Word and Sacraments*, p. 196, footnote 6.

Baptism and Conversion

> the seed of both lies hid in them by the secret operation of the Spirit.[5]

On the other hand,

> We must not deem baptism so necessary as to suppose that every one who has not had the opportunity of obtaining it has forthwith perished.[6] Children who happen to depart this life before an opportunity of immersing them in water, are not excluded from the kingdom of heaven. . . . Hence if, in omitting the sign, there is neither sloth nor contempt nor ignorance, we are safe from all danger.[7]

With this Luther would no doubt agree, but in repudiating the practice of baptism *in extremis* at the hands of a layman or a woman, Calvin shows himself to be attaching less intrinsic importance to the rite than did the Lutherans; and the Saxon Visitation Articles already quoted show that the Lutherans were well aware of this. Calvin inclines more to what was called the *obsignatory* view of baptism—that the outward rite is no more than a sign or symbol. "In baptism," he writes, "the sign is water, but the thing itself is the washing of the soul by Christ's blood";[8] and even when the sign is absent, the thing

---

[5] Book IV, Chapter XVI, 19–20.

[6] Book IV, Chapter XVI, 26.

[7] Book IV, Chapter XV, 22; mainly Beveridge's translation.

[8] Commentary on I Peter iii, 21; quoted in R. S. Wallace, *op. cit.*, p. 177.

Baptism and Regeneration

itself may be conferred by the grace of God. He believes that the work of regeneration is begun in the children of believers *ab utero* [9]—not, of course, on the ground of their natural birth but owing to their believing parentage and their being born into a Christian family; and it is on this ground that he justifies our conferring the sign upon them as soon as they are born. Such children are, as St. Paul says, already holy; they are within the covenant, they are members of Christ, sharing in the grace of adoption which God has bestowed upon their parents. But what then are we to say of the large number of baptized children of Christian parents who afterwards fall away, thus showing that they were not after all of the number of the elect? An easy way out of this difficulty would be to say that only those are regenerated in infancy who (a) are of the number of the elect and (b) are to die in infancy, while the regeneration of those elect infants who are destined to grow up to years of maturity is postponed until they come to years of understanding when personal faith is possible. The only other alternative would be to hold that all baptized children of Christian parents are regenerate, or at least that the work of regeneration has begun in them. Both these alternatives, however, seem out of accord with certain other parts of Calvin's teaching. Clearly, therefore, the Saxon Visitors were right in suspecting that there is in Calvin, as never in Luther, a certain wavering concerning the doctrine of baptismal regeneration.

[9] See Wallace, *op. cit.*, p. 193.

6

The Teaching of the Reformed Churches

LET us now pass from Calvin himself to the teaching of the Churches influenced by him. I take first the Anglican Church, which is only partly Calvinist in its tradition; and I confine myself to what is said in the XXXIX Articles and *The Book of Common Prayer*. In the former it is taught that

> baptism is a sign of regeneration or new birth whereby, as by an instrument, they that receive baptism rightly are grafted into the Church: the promises of the forgiveness of sin, and of our adoption to be the sons of God by the Holy Ghost, are visibly signed and sealed.

It is possibly not quite clear whether this allows for any hesitancy, such as we noted in Calvin, about a full doctrine of baptismal regeneration, but at least there is no hesitancy about the Order of the Administration of Baptism in *The Book of Common Prayer*. After baptism has been administered, the priest shall say, "Seeing now, dearly beloved brethren, that this child is regenerate . . .";

Baptism and Regeneration

and then, in the prayer following, "We yield thee hearty thanks, most merciful Father, that it hath pleased thee to regenerate this infant." There is no doubt, then, that the Anglican Church teaches the regeneration of infants at baptism.

Since I cannot take time to deal with them all, I shall choose from the Confessions of the Reformed Churches the one I know best, namely, the Westminster Confession. It reads on the whole not unlike the XXXIX Articles on this matter. The concept of regeneration is still mainly associated with baptism—and therefore in practice with baptism in infancy, since adult baptism would be comparatively rare in those days. We read that

> Elect infants, dying in infancy, are regenerated and saved by Christ through the Holy Spirit. . . . So also are all other elect persons who are incapable of being outwardly called by the ministry of the Word

—the reference of the last clause being doubtless to mental defectives. To the writers of this Confession, who had followed the first Reformers in abolishing the "limbo of the infants," there were only what they called "two places for souls after death"—heaven and hell. But since they were unwilling to believe that all infants dying in infancy and all mental defectives were lost, they were not deterred from allowing that regeneration can take place in infancy and in mental defectives by the supposed Reformation

Baptism and Conversion

principle that there can be no regeneration without conscious faith.

Note, however, that this Confession clearly teaches, as Calvin had not so clearly taught, that only *elect* infants are regenerated. If, however, as the Confession also teaches, all infants born of Christian parents are holy and are made members incorporate of the Body of Christ (i.e., of the Church) at baptism, how then can they not be regenerate? The answer is given in terms of a new distinction, hardly known to the Medieval Church and appearing first in Luther, between the Church visible and the Church invisible. This is most clearly stated in the Westminster Larger Catechism, where the visible Church is defined as "a society made up of all such as in all ages and places of the world do profess the true religion, and of their children," [1] and the invisible Church as "the whole number of the elect," [2] and where it is then definitely stated that "All that hear the gospel, and live in the visible church, are not saved; but only they who are true members of the church invisible." [3] But does the Confession mean to teach that not all elect infants are regenerated in infancy and at baptism, but only those who die in infancy, the regeneration of other elect infants being delayed until personal faith can be imparted to them, so that regeneration in infancy is, as it were, the exception

[1] Q. 62.
[2] Q. 64.
[3] Q. 61.

Baptism and Regeneration

rather than the rule? This would perhaps seem to be the logical working out of the position, as also of Calvin's own position, but it is certainly never clearly said. Nor am I sure whether there is anything bearing on this point in the statement that "the grace promised (in baptism) is not only offered, but really exhibited and conferred by the Holy Ghost, to such (whether of age or infants) as that grace belongeth unto, according to the counsel of God's own will, in his appointed time."[4]

Many further examples of Calvinist teaching on these matters are collected in Heppe's well-known compendium of *Reformed Dogmatics*. To cite one example only, the theologian Heidegger writes that it may be assumed that the elect who die in infancy

> are regenerated and sanctified even in their mother's womb, and therefore baptism is the sign of a regeneration already made and persevering right up to death.

Yet

> not for the children of believing parents one and all, but only for the elect is baptism the sign of regeneration and universal spiritual grace. Although it is right and godly, in the case of individual children of this kind, to have good hopes of the judgement in love, in the case of all of them it is not so.[5]

[4] Westminster Confession, Chapter XXVIII.
[5] *Op. cit.*, English translation, pp. 622f.

Baptism and Conversion

And here, because time will not permit me to deal with the Zwinglian teaching in detail, I shall simply remark that a somewhat more generous hope is allowed by the following statement from the First Helvetic Confession of 1536:

> In this holy bath we baptize our children, because it would be wrong that we should exclude from the community of the people of God those born of us (the people of God) who through the divine Word are appointed thereto, and whose election is to be presumed (*zu vermuthen, praesumendum*).[6]

I think to a Calvinist this would be an unwarrantable presumption.

Clearly in all these Calvinist documents everything turns on election; the Saxon Visitors were right about that. Not on faith, not on baptism, but on election. All who are elect must be regenerated and saved, whether in adult life or in infancy, and therefore with or without faith, and also with or without baptism. It is also virtually taken for granted that not all who die in infancy are thus elect; and this was to cause much searching of heart within the Reformed Churches in the nineteenth century, necessitating in Scotland the passing of two Declaratory Acts

[6] Article XXII.

Baptism and Regeneration

which are now among the standards of the Church of Scotland, one in 1879 and the other in 1892, to assure us that "it is not required to be believed that any who die in infancy are lost."

7

The Teaching of the Baptist Churches

To complete this hurried historical survey, a further word is necessary about the teaching of certain Churches of post-Reformation origin, especially about the Baptist Churches. If their position need not detain us long, it is only because it can be very simply stated, standing as it does for a frank simplification of the whole problem such as the other Churches would characterize as a cutting of the Gordian knot. We have seen how the other Protestant Churches have experienced some degree of difficulty in reconciling their practice of infant baptism, associated as it had always been with regeneration, with the Reformation principle of salvation by faith alone. The Baptist Churches have solved this problem by the simple expedient of discontinuing the practice of infant baptism altogether. It will suffice here to quote from the earliest Baptist Confession, that printed at Amsterdam in 1611. We read in Article XIII of that Confession that

> every Church is to receive all its members by baptism upon the confession of their faith and sins,

Baptism and Regeneration

wrought by the preaching of the Gospel, according to the primitive institution and practice. And therefore Churches constituted in any other manner or of any other persons, are not according to Christ's testament.

And in Article XIV that

> Baptism, or washing with water, is the outward manifestation of dying unto sin and walking in newness of life: and therefore in no wise appertaineth to infants.

These Churches thus follow the tradition in closely connecting baptism with regeneration, and it is precisely for this reason that they refuse to baptize infants, since they hold that infants cannot be regenerated. On the other hand, this connection means for them only that none must be baptized save those who by confession give evidence of having already been regenerated. They refuse to ascribe the regenerative efficacy to baptism itself, nor do they hold that baptism is necessary to regeneration, but only that it is the duty of all who believe themselves regenerate to submit themselves afterwards to baptism.

But there are other Churches of post-Reformation origin and—perhaps even more important—there is a certain body of opinion within many Protestant Churches, which would solve what is essentially the same problem in what is virtually the opposite way. We Christians, they say,

Baptism and Conversion

must indeed baptize our babies, but we must not understand such baptism either as itself conferring regeneration or as following upon a regeneration already present; since not until years of discretion are reached can any be spoken of as regenerate Christians.

8

An Attempted Conclusion

HAVING now put in brief summary the teaching of the various Christian Churches in the West concerning the relation of baptism to regeneration, I must next try to say what I myself believe. There are of course many important aspects of the Christian doctrine of baptism concerning which I have said nothing and do not propose to say anything, because they do not immediately affect the subject of these lectures, which is the nature of the process by which an individual may be said to become a Christian. Towards the end I shall develop more fully my own view as to the nature of this process, but meanwhile I shall present it only in relation to the question of baptism.

Referring then to the terms of Bishop Neill's statement, I am sure we must hold to the view that "Christian life begins at baptism." I cannot doubt that this is the universal New Testament view. Baptism is the rite which marks the incorporation of the individual into the Body of Christ, his adoption into the household of God. As clearly, and by the same sign, it is the rite of regeneration, of being born again into the newness of the Christian life.

Baptism and Conversion

By the same sign also it is the rite of purification, of forgiveness and the washing away of sin.

This means that the outward rite and the inward renewal normally and properly accompany one another, but this leaves open the question of the precise nature of the relation between the two; and about that I must now say something. To begin with, we must say that the grace of regeneration is not—and I borrow the phrase from the Westminster Confession—so "inseparably annexed" to the washing with water that none can be regenerated who have not been subjected to such washing. This is allowed in one way or another by all the traditions. Even the Roman Church, which begins by affirming that baptism is necessary to salvation, goes on to speak of a "baptism of desire" and of certain graces which can by way of exception take the place of baptism.[1] But it is Calvin and the Reformed tradition which speak most clearly on this matter, and I should be in full agreement with them. Furthermore the Reformed tradition warns us against believing—and again I quote from the Westminster Confession—that "all who are baptized are undoubtedly regenerated";[2] and with this also we must certainly agree. The outward rite taken by itself is nothing. The washing with water accomplishes nothing by itself alone. It is significant only when it accompanies the effective recep-

---

[1] Cf. Cardinal Gasparri's *Catholic Catechism*, Q. 360 and footnote.
[2] Chapter XXVIII.

Baptism and Regeneration

tion of the initiate into the Christian community, which is the Body of Christ. On the other hand we must believe that, when so accompanied, the outward rite becomes a vital part of the efficacious instrument of renewal. We must not regard the washing with water merely as a pleasant formality, or as having only subjective efficacy for the recipient. Karl Barth, while rejecting the teaching concerning the efficacy of the rite which he ascribes to Romanism, Lutheranism and Anglicanism, nevertheless welcomes what he calls the "realism" of these traditions in not being deterred by the fear of giving way to "magic," from recognizing that something quite definite and specific is accomplished through it. But his view is that baptism has to do, not with the *causa salutis*, the cause of salvation, but only with the *cognitio salutis*, the assurance of salvation.[3] But Oscar Cullmann, in his reply to Barth, has, I think, conclusively shown that there is no New Testament warrant for such a view. I quote the following:

> I find no passage in which it is said or hinted that we have to seek in *cognitio* the special content of the act of baptism. . . . On the contrary what happens in the act of baptism is clearly defined in the decisive Pauline texts I Cor. xii, 13 and Gal. iii, 27–28 as a setting within the Body of Christ. God sets a man within, *not merely informs him that He sets him within*, the Body of Christ.[4]

[3] *Die kirchliche Lehre von der Taufe.*
[4] *Baptism in the New Testament*, English translation, p. 31.

Baptism and Conversion

The Body of Christ, into which the individual is received by baptism, is of course the *koinonia*, the community of the faithful, the Christian Church. And the point I am most anxious to make is that *unless* the washing with water accompanies, and is accompanied by, effective reception into the Christian community, it is void of all significance. It would therefore be a gross abuse of the sacrament if we should baptize babies who are not the children of Christian parents, who neither were born nor are to be brought up in a Christian home or within a Christian congregation. It is through his Christian nurture that the grace of God reaches the child—through the home into which he is born and the Christian community into which he is received. If he is not effectively received into such a community, if there is *nobody* who is caring for his Christian upbringing, then the outward ritual—the washing with water—is not Christian baptism at all, and means nothing. On the other hand I should agree with those theologians of the Reformed tradition who hold that a child born into a Christian home is in a true sense a Christian child from birth—*ab utero*, as they said. Such children are "holy unto the Lord." They are "within the Covenant," and "the promise is also to them." Baptism is the divinely ordained ritual which sets a seal upon their Covenant status, and by which they are received into the wider Christian community.

What is important, then, is that our children should be brought up from infancy as Christian children. We

Baptism and Regeneration

should teach them that they already belong to Christ, and we should address them as those who belong to Him. We should not encourage them to look upon themselves as still outside. Let me quote another eloquent passage from Frederick Denison Maurice—from his book on *The Kingdom of Christ*. He refuses to evade the issue here involved by relying upon a distinction between the Church visible and the Church invisible, and by saying that our children are at baptism received only into the former. He characterizes as follows the teaching to which he is opposed, and which he ascribes to certain "modern Protestant evangelicals":

> that there are two kingdoms of Christ, one real and spiritual, the other outward and visible. It is highly desirable, perhaps necessary, that young as well as old should be admitted into the latter. Baptism is the appointed means of admission. What are the privileges of the Gentile Court into which, by this ordinance, we are received, they do not precisely determine. Possibly some grace is communicated at baptism; or if not, the blessings of being permitted to hear preaching, and of obtaining Christian education, are great, and may be turned to greater use hereafter. But the important point of all is this, to press upon men that till they have been consciously converted they are not members of Christ or children of God. Some disciples of this school believe that these words may be applied to baptized people *in a sense*; but if you desire to know in what

Baptism and Conversion

> sense, the answers are so vague and indeterminate
> as to leave a painful impression upon the mind.[5]

I agree with Maurice in thinking this teaching unfortunate, and I am glad that there is no mention of any distinction corresponding to that between "two kingdoms" in the Order for the Administration of the Sacrament of Baptism in the *Book of Common Order* of the Church of Scotland. There the administrant says this in the opening address to the congregation:

> Though little children do not understand these
> things, yet is the promise also to them. They are
> heirs of the covenant of grace; and in holy Baptism God brings them into the family and household of faith, and makes them members of Christ,
> and citizens of the kingdom of heaven.

And after the sacrament has been administered, the minister says this:

> According to Christ's commandment this child
> is now received into the membership of the holy
> Catholic Church, and is engaged to confess the
> faith of Christ crucified, and to be His faithful
> soldier and servant unto his (or her) life's end.

If now the question be pressed, "How can a child be a Christian before the age when personal faith is possible?"

[5] *Op. cit.*, Vol. I, pp. 301f. (Part II, Chapter IV).

Baptism and Regeneration

I would answer that we cannot posit any age, however young, when the disposition of faith may not already have begun to appear. When a child is born and baptized into the household of faith, and acquiesces in the manner of his upbringing, the disposition of faith, by the grace of God operating through his Christian home, is already being formed within him. As Calvin puts it, he has "the seed of faith" in him, and that is all that is then required. He is, I would say, what God wants him to be at that age and stage. He is not a mature Christian, but God does not want him to be that yet; and he may already be just the kind of Christian that God wants him to be at that stage. Indeed he is probably a better Christian for his age than most of us are for our later ages. "Jesus said, Let the children come to me, and do not hinder them; for of such is the kingdom of heaven. And he laid his hands on them." [6] Calvin insists that we must give full weight to the words "of such is the kingdom of heaven." Not, he says, that they belong to that kingdom *by nature*, or in virtue of natural propagation, but only by being born into the household of faith. It was not of all children that our Lord spoke these words, but only of the children of Abraham, who were born within the Covenant.

Baptized children thus belong to Christ, but the sad fact is that many of them, as they grow up to maturity, fall into behaving as if they did not belong to Him, and often altogether repudiate His ownership. Yet this hap-

[6] Matthew xix, 14–15.

Baptism and Conversion

pens also to some of those who by their own personal decision have committed themselves to Christ in later years. But in both cases our approach and address should not be: "You do not yet belong to Christ, but you should now commit yourself to Him"; but rather, "You were united to Christ in your baptism; turn back to Him to whom you belong." In the context of the passage already quoted from him, F. D. Maurice answers the objection that many who have been baptized are now living sinful lives, so that they cannot really be within the Covenant. Yes, he says, they are certainly living in sin, but in what sin? The sin is that, being within the Covenant, they are living as if they were not.

I hope, then, that I have made clear the sense in which I believe that Christian life begins at baptism. Later I shall return to this matter, setting it then within a wider context.

II

Pre-Christian Conversion

9

Conversion to a Religion
and Conversion within a Religion

WHAT I have so far had to say has revolved mainly round the concept of regeneration, but what I have next to say will be mainly concerned with the concept of conversion. Here the first point to notice is that there are at least two—and as we proceed, we shall have to ask whether there are not more than two—classes of event to which the word is familiarly applied.

When used in a religious sense and without further context, the word suggests to our Protestant ears either one of two things which sometimes go together and sometimes do not. It may mean a change-over from one religious allegiance to another, as when we speak of a man's being a convert from paganism to Islam, from Judaism to Christianity, or from Anglicanism to Romanism. Or it may mean a crisis in which a man "comes to himself," as did the Prodigal Son, and for the first time faces up to the realities of his moral and spiritual situation. The difference is that in the first case the man comes to believe something to be true which he had not hitherto believed to be true, or finds himself challenged by an en-

Baptism and Conversion

tirely new situation; while in the other case he is for the first time seriously adjusting himself to something the truth of which he had never doubted, or to a situation in which he had always known himself to stand. The two, as I have said, very often go together. Conversion to another cult means in a very large proportion of cases that a man is then for the first time taking serious thought for his spiritual condition. On the other hand, each also frequently happens independently of the other. Some transferences of allegiance, for instance, as when a devout Jew is converted to Christianity, or a devout Anglican to Romanism, have been antedated by a very complete experience of self-commitment within their own earlier faith. Some Jews and Moslems have been as much at peace with their Jewish or Moslem consciences as any Christian with his Christian conscience before God. And conversely we are all very familiar with conversion crises of the second kind occurring quite apart from any transference of allegiance from the faith of a man's own tradition and upbringing.

10

Conversion within the Pagan Religions

LET US then, before coming to distinctively Christian ground, consider what may be said about pre-Christian or non-Christian conversion. There is a considerable literature to guide us. Over a quarter of a century ago the late Principal A. C. Underwood of Leeds published a book with the title *Conversion: Christian and Non-Christian*. The posthumous book on *Conversion* by W. P. Paterson has a chapter on pre-Christian conversions. There is a French treatise by Allier with the title *Psychologie de la Conversion chez les peuples non-civilisés*. And perhaps most useful of all is A. D. Nock's *Conversion: from Alexander the Great to Augustine of Hippo*. Profiting from these books, we may ask how far conversion experiences have been or are enjoyed outside Christianity.

Perhaps we shall naturally think first of those solemn initiation ceremonies which are a feature of even the crudest pagan cults, when the youth of the tribe, on reaching adolescence, are made to undergo an elaborate ritual by which they are confirmed in the tribal tradition. But while this ritual does undoubtedly give rise in their

Baptism and Conversion

minds to exalted emotions of a religious kind, there is little evidence of its being associated with anything like repentance. There is no turning from past indifference to whole-hearted allegiance, but only something like initiation into further knowledge and further privilege; so that I am sure it would be misleading to speak here of conversion.

The case is somewhat different when we turn to the many instances occurring in the ancient religions of men being initiated into specialized cults, such as were not part of the common tradition of their people, but promised a certain added blessedness to those who took part in them. A notable example is provided by the Eleusinian and other mysteries in ancient Greece, but of these Nock says that they "were as a rule supplements rather than alternatives to ancestral piety," [1] and that the feelings we associate with conversion were seldom excited by them. The same is true of the many instances in the ancient world in which an adherent of an ancestral cult was attracted by another cult; what usually happened was that he added a new god to his existing pantheon and another worship to his existing devotions. This led, says Nock,

> not to any definite crossing of religious frontiers, in which an old spiritual home was left for a new one once and for all, but to men's having one foot on each side of a fence which was cultural and not creedal. They led to an acceptance of new

[1] *Op. cit.*, p. 12.

Pre-Christian Conversion

worships as useful supplements and not as substitutes, and they did not involve the taking of a new way of life in place of the old. This we may call adhesion in contradistinction to conversion.[2]

This means that in the ancient traditional religions (before the rise of the great religious systems and missionary religions) conversion can hardly be spoken of in either of our two senses—either as transference of religious allegiance or as self-surrender and coming to oneself. Yet Professor Nock allows that the case is somewhat different with reference to the Orphic sodalities in ancient Greece. Orphism had close connection with some of the philosophic schools, and the surprising fact is that it is in these schools, rather than in the traditional religions, that we find the first clear emergence of the idea of conversion. Most of these schools did call men to a new and radically different way of life, such as demanded a complete change of heart; a renunciation of the old man and the acceptance of a severe new discipline. Of none was this more true than of the Stoics, and indeed it might be said of the Stoics that they were the earliest teachers anywhere to work out a doctrine of conversion in set terms—a doctrine which has some remarkable points of resemblance to later Christian teaching. The word "conversion" itself derives from them. *Conversio* was the usual translation among the Roman Stoics of the technical terms *metabole*,

[2] *Op. cit.*, pp. 16f.

Baptism and Conversion

metastrophe and *ektrope* used by their Greek masters, who taught them that when a man forsook his old way of life to embrace the Stoic way (*agoge*), a complete change was accomplished in him. The change was indeed preceded by a long preparation, which they called *prokope*, but was itself quite sudden and abrupt, there being essentially no middle ground between folly and wisdom. The good, they said, cannot be attained by addition (*accessio*). Cicero quotes two analogies to illustrate the nature of conversion; that of a man who has fallen into deep water and gradually rises towards the surface, yet quite suddenly reaches the surface and in a single moment finds himself able to breathe; and that of a puppy who is born blind and gradually advances towards the power of vision, but then quite suddenly discovers that he can see things.[3] When, however, a man has once been converted, he enjoys complete assurance of his own changed condition, and from that condition he cannot again fall away. These are all positions which, as we shall see, have frequently been occupied by Christian theologians—that a man either is or is not converted, that there is no middle ground; that consequently, however gradually conversion may be led up to (so that in that sense it is not sudden), the actual conversion itself must take place in a single indivisible moment; that when a man has been converted, he enjoys complete assurance of his changed state; and that, when once this change has taken place in him, he can never fall away. There seems little doubt that more

[3] *De finibus*, 14, 48.

Pre-Christian Conversion

than anywhere else in the West it was in the Greek philosophic schools that men enjoyed critical conversion experiences of this kind.

But if we turn from the West to the great religions of India, to the great movements of the spirit that developed against the general background of traditional Hindu culture and piety—to the *Bhakti-marga* and Buddhism especially—we find a remarkable resemblance to this Stoic teaching. Here also the conversion experience occupies the centre of the picture and is conceived, as later by St. John, as regeneration or new birth. In Buddhism, as in Roman Christianity, the converts fell into two classes, those who forsook the world for the monastic life and those who, accepting a lower ideal, remained in home and secular calling. There seems no doubt that many Hindus and Buddhists did, and still do, enjoy a critical experience of release, of peace of mind, and of what in our modern jargon is called "psychological integration," and also an assurance of salvation which, on its subjective side, is very difficult to distinguish from many of the conversion experiences collected by William James in his *Varieties of Religious Experience*. "It is not open to doubt," writes Principal Underwood, "that Buddha himself was a twice-born soul." Indeed, we can say quite generally that if conversion is to be defined as a personal crisis in which a man, leaving behind him a life of drift or of self-centred indulgence, completely surrenders himself to the highest he knows, then it is a familiar experience in India.

11

Conversion in the Old Testament

LET US now briefly ask, before going on to specifically Christian ground, how it was with the Hebrew piety of Old Testament and pre-Christian times.

Every Israelite was regarded as being within the Covenant. The children also were within it. All male babies were subjected to the rite of circumcision a week after birth, and were thus sealed as being within the Covenant—in the same way that baptism was afterwards held to seal the children of Christians as being within the Church.

It was, however, the conviction and contention of the great prophets of the eighth and seventh centuries B.C. that the Israelitish nation was now in large measure in a state of apostasy, having violated the terms of the Covenant. Hence almost their whole message consists in a call to repentance. The nation is exhorted to *re*pent, to *re*turn, to turn *back*. It is a restoration that is thought of. All the terms used imply that by such contrition the nation does not for the first time enter into covenant-relationship with God, but that it returns to a relationship it had formerly enjoyed. Moreover it is the nation as a whole that is sum-

Pre-Christian Conversion

moned to repent. It is a corporate conversion, a revival of the nation, that is spoken of. One example may be quoted from Ezekiel:

> Then will I sprinkle clean water upon you, and ye shall be clean; from all your filthiness, and from all your idols, will I cleanse you. A new heart also will I give you, and a new spirit also will I put within you; and I will take away the stony heart out of your flesh, and I will give you an heart of flesh. And I will put my spirit within you, and cause you to walk in my statutes, and ye shall keep my judgements and do them. And ye shall dwell in the land I gave to your fathers: and ye shall be my people, and I will be your God. . . . Then shall you remember your own evil ways, and your doings that were not good, and shall loathe yourselves in your own sight for your iniquities and for your abominations.[1]

Of course the nation is made up of individuals, and the nation can be changed only if the hearts of many individuals are changed. Yet the sins to be repented of are essentially national sins, and the change required is in that sense a change in the temper of the nation as distinct from a number of separate and unrelated changes in the hearts of so many individuals.

But do we also read in the pages of the Old Testament of individual conversions in the sense made familiar to

[1] Ezekiel xxxvi, 25–31.

Baptism and Conversion

us by later usage? Perhaps we think first of the fifty-first psalm. If the psalm be ascribed to David, then this would indeed be a case of individual conversion, though not indeed of a first turning to God, but rather of a return. But the prevailing view of scholars is that the psalm is to be read not as an utterance of David or any other individual, but as an utterance of the nation. As early as Theodore of Mopsuestia the view was taken that it is a prayer of Israel in Babylonia, a confession of national sin and a plea for restoration from the Exile. Robertson Smith, G. R. Driver and numerous other scholars follow this view. Israel, they say, is here personified as it is in the Servant of the Lord passages in Deutero-Isaiah. Indeed the closing verses read: "Do good in thy good pleasure unto Zion: build thou the walls of Jerusalem. Then shalt thou be pleased with the sacrifices of righteousness, with burnt-offering and whole burnt-offering: they shall offer bullocks upon thine altar"—which seems plainly to refer to the rebuilding of the Temple after the Exile.

It is also important to notice that where the word conversion has been most commonly used with reference to individuals in the Old Testament has been in connection with the call of the prophets. We think of how Samuel was called, and of how Isaiah, Amos, Jeremiah and Ezekiel were called. We cannot doubt that each of these calls was an overwhelming individual experience. But what we must note is that each was a call and appointment to a holy office—to the office and work of a prophet; and not

Pre-Christian Conversion

a call by which all were called. It was thus more like what we mean by a call to the ministry than like what the Calvinists mean by effectual calling or what evangelicals mean by conversion. And we shall presently be noting that this call to a more specialized duty and discipline is what the Middle Ages, and the Romans to this day, most usually speak of as *conversio* and *vocatio*. Moreover in these Old Testament cases the sense of *national* apostasy is very strong. "I am a man of unclean lips," Isaiah said on the occasion of his call, "and I dwell in the midst of a people of unclean lips."

As to the Judaism of a later period, we need note only that according to Jewish scholars the emphasis there was almost entirely upon early training. All children were brought up within the Covenant and taught to think of themselves as being within it, so that no later experience of a critical kind was required of them; which, however, is not to say that it did not frequently happen.

12

Conversion to a Faith following on Conversion within another Faith

AND HERE, before proceeding further, we may raise another question. If we understand conversion in the sense of a transference of allegiance, then we must say that history records many instances of men's having had two conversions, first to one religious tradition, and then from that to another. But if we understand conversion in the other sense of a "coming to oneself" after a life of self-indulgence, we must likewise say that there are many instances of men's having had this experience within their own ancestral tradition and afterwards transferring their allegiance to another faith. Some men, for instance, who have been converted from an Eastern religion to Christianity were already leading lives of a devoutness and consecration which would put many of their new associates to shame, having passed through an experience, as it were of second birth, within their native religious tradition before the Gospel was preached to them. Again, John Henry Newman had made his peace with God, and would be said to be converted in the one sense, before being con-

Pre-Christian Conversion

verted, in the other sense, to Romanism. Another case to consider is that of those who responded to the call of our Lord in the days of His flesh. Some of these were doubtless turning to Him from a life of apostasy; but others were already at peace with themselves and with God on the basis of the Old Testament revelation before being converted to the obedience of the Gospel. No doubt we should say that in Paul's case the two conversions were united in a single experience—that he had never, devout and pious Jew as he was, found peace until he found it in Christ. But I have sufficiently made my point, which is that we must distinguish between two or—as it now appears—even three kinds of conversion; namely, conversion as a crisis of self-surrender, conversion as transference of religious allegiance, and conversion as call to an office or discipline such as is required of only a few. Perhaps one reason why we are so apt to conflate these meanings into one is that we think of the cases of St. Paul and St. Augustine as the typical cases of conversion. But neither was typical. St. Paul was converted from one obedience to another, and St. Augustine's conversion was in no small part of the kind denominated by the prevailing medieval usage of the word—to the celibate, if not quite to the monastic life. Or we think of John Wesley's conversion, meaning by that the incident in Aldersgate Street on May 24th, 1738. But that also has been the subject of much debate, there being those who would prefer to apply the word conversion to what took place in 1725,

Baptism and Conversion

when he was preparing at Oxford for his ordination. One Wesleyan authority writes:

> If by conversion we mean a turning from a course of sinful disobedience to one of reverent penitential service and devotion, it cannot with strict accuracy be affirmed that what occurred in the little room in Aldersgate Street, London, is correctly described as Wesley's conversion. Before that event Wesley was not a blasphemer or a persecutor; it cannot be said that he was ever such a one. But the passage in his career at Oxford, when he shook himself free from all indifference, and when he entered upon a course of earnestness in the government of his life, may with some exactness claim to have in it the true elements of conversion.[1]

At all events it is difficult to think of the experience usually known as his conversion as that in which John Wesley first "became a Christian."

[1] Richard Green, *The Conversion of John Wesley* (New edition, Epworth Press, 1937), p. 11.

III

THE TEACHING OF THE CHRISTIAN
CHURCHES ABOUT CONVERSION

13

The Medieval and Roman Teaching

LET us now pass to distinctively Christian ground, and let us begin with the teaching of the Medieval and Roman Church. As we have already seen, it is here taught that baptism must be followed by confirmation, which is a separate sacrament, the second of the seven; the distinction between the two being that in baptism sins are remitted, while in confirmation the graces of the Holy Spirit are conferred. Sins committed after baptism must be confessed and the further sacrament of penance administered in respect of them.

What then of conversion? I once asked one of the most distinguished of living Roman thinkers what he understood by the word. He replied at once, "when we use the word in my communion, we usually have in mind a call to the monastic life." This was undoubtedly the prevailing usage in the pre-Reformation Church. Or rather the *conversi* were *one* class of those who were so called, namely, those who in adult life renounced the world, manifesting *conversio a saeculo ad vitam religiosam*; as distinct from the *oblati*, the oblates, who were "offered" to a monastery by their parents in childhood. There were and are, how-

Baptism and Conversion

ever, other usages of the term. It was used of the evangelization of pagans—the "conversion" of Constantine was spoken of. It was and is also frequently applied to the return of Christians from heresy or schism to orthodoxy; so that Roman Catholics will speak freely of the conversion of Protestants to Romanism, as for example Newman. Yet it remains true that the principal traditional use of the word has been in connection with *vocatio*—with the call to lead the religious or monastic as distinct from the secular life. And of course in the pre-Reformation Church calling or vocation was chiefly spoken of in connection with the call to the religious life—in the sense in which we expect a theological student to know himself called to the holy ministry. *The Catholic Encyclopaedia* in its article on "Vocation" says that calling is primarily "to the ecclesiastical life or the evangelical counsels," though "an effectual calling to believe" is also spoken of.

I wonder whether it might not be true to say that when a critical experience of the kind familiar to Protestant evangelicals under the name of conversion is had by one who has been brought up from childhood within the discipline of the Roman Church, it is generally interpreted as a call to take monastic vows or their equivalent. Luther, I think, makes it clear that this was how he understood conversion before his break with Rome. Yet we must add that according to Roman teaching the religious life, though sharply distinguished from the life of ordinary Christians, is not held necessarily and in all cases to imply

The Christian Churches about Conversion

retirement from the world into a monastery or nunnery. In its widest sense it means rather a life which obeys what are called the "evangelical counsels" or "counsels of perfection," such as are not obligatory on all Christians. It is allowed that these may be obeyed by some without retiring from the world. But such a course is discouraged as being fraught with dangers.[1]

[1] Cf. *The Catholic Encyclopaedia*: article on "Vocation."

14

The Lutheran Teaching

WHAT change did the Reformation bring in this way of speaking and thinking? We may say, to begin with, that nothing lay closer to the root of Luther's departure from the teaching in which he had been brought up than his refusal to accept the distinction between a secular and a "religious" class of Christians. To him *all* Christians are called to obey *all* the counsels of God; and this is possible because in his view retirement from the world is not an evangelical counsel at all. Thus the Reformation introduces a new doctrine of vocation, allowing for an unlimited variety of secular callings.[1] This meant at the same time that Luther could no longer use the term conversion in its customary medieval sense. Indeed the word cannot be said to be a key term in Luther's discourse. He does use it frequently, but he fails to define its relation to the other terms he uses. *The Encyclopaedia of Religion and Ethics* notes that even during his lifetime there were those who regarded his guidance in the matter as defective. "To questions in regard to the time and

[1] See W. R. Forrester, *Christian Vocation*, Chapter XII, "The Doctrine of Vocation as Restored by Calvin and Luther."

The Christian Churches about Conversion

manner of conversion, his answers were said to be indecisive and incomplete." [2] At all events he refuses to use the term as meaning a call to the monastic life, and, though it may not be clear just what stage in spiritual growth he usually has in mind when he employs it, he is quite clear that no man can be a Christian unless he be converted. He believed that as full a self-commitment as the Roman Church expected of monks and nuns must be expected of every citizen. He would have no double standard. That is the genius of the Reformation, and it is the main point Luther is desirous of making about conversion.

It is sometimes charged that what Protestantism in effect did, in abolishing the double standard, was to reduce all Christian life to the level of the lower. In view of the little that is often expected of Church members in some modern Protestant communities, we cannot say that the charge is devoid of all justification. On the other hand, if one looks back to the days of our Protestant forefathers, one realizes that never anywhere has there been a more dedicated and demanding Christian piety than was exemplified in the lives of large numbers of ordinary Christians engaged in their ordinary tasks. The Puritan rigorism of England and New England, whatever its grievous faults, was as strict in its own different way as any medieval monastic rule. Read also such books as Marshall on *Justification*, Guthrie's *The Christian's Great Interest*,

[2] Article on "Certainty (Religious)," Vol. 3.

Baptism and Conversion

John Newton's *Cardiphonia*, Law's *Serious Call to a Devout and Holy Life*, *The Diary of Mrs. Kitty Trevelyan* and Samuel Rutherford's *Letters*, if you desire to understand the Protestant version of the devoted life. I remember that when in my schooldays I used to read such medieval books as Thomas à Kempis' *The Imitation of Christ*, there was an element running through them that puzzled me, and many phrases and allusions that I could not interpret or apply to my own case. It was long afterwards that I understood the reason why. A Kempis wrote only for monks and nuns. The French historian Pourrat has written in his work on *La spiritualité chrétienne* that in the patristic period and throughout a great part of the Middle Ages "no books of devotion were composed for Christians living 'in the world,'" because in those days "all who posed to take the quest for perfection seriously became monks—either by retiring to the desert or cloister, or by practising domestic asceticism of a monastic kind."[3] The discipline described and proposed in the Protestant books I have mentioned is not of the monastic kind, but in its own kind it is no less demanding.

I have said that, unlike the tradition of his upbringing, Luther will agree to use the term conversion only in a sense in which it is applicable to all Christians, but that he is far from definite about the stage or event in the progress of the Christian life to which he would now transfer it. I have nowhere seen his usage fully investi-

[3] Vol. I, pp. 9f.

The Christian Churches about Conversion

gated, but I would tentatively venture the opinion that, while on the one hand he distinguishes it as a later event from regeneration at baptism, on the other hand he does not conceive it, in the manner of later pietism and evangelicalism, as a single unrepeatable later event, but rather identifies it with the confession and absolution which should follow each commission of post-baptismal sin. Sometimes he seems to use the word "justification" in this way, distinguishing it from regeneration. In his Small Catechism, having dealt with the sacrament of baptism as regenerative, he proceeds to deal with *poenitentia*—penitence or penance—which to the Romans had been a further sacrament; and he says that it comprehends two parts, first confession, and second "that we receive absolution from the father confessor, as from God Himself, in no wise doubting, but firmly believing, that our sins are thereby forgiven before God in heaven." It would seem on the whole that every time a sinner confesses and is given absolution, he is said to be converted anew.

This view seems also to be implied in the later Lutheran formularies. The Formula of Concord (1576–1584) has much to say about conversion and, though I find what it says very difficult to interpret, it seems on the whole to follow this view. Similarly the Augsburg Confession. In the German version of the Confession it is said that absolution is given, with remission of sins, to penitents "every time they come to repentance" (*zur Busse kommen*); but in the Latin version we read *quo-*

Baptism and Conversion

cunque tempore dum convertuntur—"every time they are converted." Further, the Formula of Concord explicitly condemns the view that in the Biblical usage the verb *iustificare* is not equivalent to the verb *absolvere*.[4] There seems then little doubt about the identification.

Before passing on to Calvinism there are three further points to be noted about the Lutheran teaching.

First, it is taught that every Christian, after due confession and absolution, should have complete assurance that he has received forgiveness and is in a state of grace. Rome taught and still teaches otherwise. According to the Decrees of the Council of Trent "no one can know with a certainty of belief, which cannot be subject to doubt, that he has obtained the grace of God."[5] But Luther writes in his Commentary on Galatians:

> It is very expedient for the godly to know that they have the Holy Spirit. This I say to confute the pernicious doctrine of the Papists, which taught that no man certainly knows, although his life be never so upright and blameless, whether he be in the favour of God or no.[6]

And the Formula of Concord lays it down that Christians

> ought not to doubt *either* of the righteousness which is imputed to them through faith *or* of

[4] Article III, 7.
[5] VI, 12.
[6] On Chapter IV, verse 6; English translation of 1575.

The Christian Churches about Conversion

their eternal salvation, but rather are they to be firmly convinced that, for Christ's sake . . . they have God reconciled to them.[7]

I may quote this also from Friedrich Heiler, himself a convert from Romanism to Lutheranism:

> That which the theologians and popes of the Middle Ages had so tabooed—the assurance of salvation in the consciousness of the redeemed—became for Luther the heart and core of the Christian faith. It was not through some special revelation that this assurance was bestowed upon the recipients of God's mercy—that the Roman Church recognized—no, it was God's word that cannot lie and His inviolable promise of mercy which gave to every soul of man that believes, this assurance.[8]

Second, and on the other hand, and this time in agreement with Rome, the teaching that "once saved, always saved" is definitely rejected. The Formula of Concord explicitly condemns the opinion that faith cannot be lost "even if a man should sin *sciens, volensque* (wittingly and willingly)," and "fall into adultery and other crimes, and persevere in the same." [9] This is of course held in conjunction with the teaching that not even the commission

[7] Article III, 6.
[8] *The Spirit of Worship*, English translation, p. 176.
[9] Article IV.

Baptism and Conversion

of the most serious sins will imperil a man's salvation if, being duly repentant of them and remembering his baptism, he continues to believe that the imputed righteousness avails for his justification.[10]

Third, whereas it is taught that baptism effects (*efficiat*) *regeneratio* and *renovatio*,[11] and that infants who are baptized are thus "born again," it is at the same time held that regeneration is not then completed, and that in this life it is never completed; and the phrase *credentes, quatenus renati sunt*, "believers in so far as they are born again," is frequently used in the Formula of Concord. Complete regeneration is thus not necessary to salvation, but only a beginning of it.

[10] *Formula of Concord*, Article III, 7.
[11] *Formula of Concord*, Article IV.

15

The Reformed Teaching

LET US pass now to Calvinism. As regards the point last mentioned, we have already seen that Calvin agrees with Luther, saying that regeneration, though begun in baptism, "is not completed in a moment, in a day, or a year,"[1] but is a continuous process throughout the whole of life. But we have seen also that, whereas Luther tends to think of *poenitentia* as coming later than baptismal regeneration, being associated with later confession and absolution, as in the Roman Church, Calvin identifies the two—"*uno verbo poenitentiam interpretor regenerationem,*"[2] How then does Calvin use the term conversion? I find it even less of a key term for him than it is for Luther. "It is quite certain," he writes, "that the whole sum of the gospel can be contained under these two heads —penitence and remission of sins."[3] These then are his key terms. But penitence is to him the same as regeneration; and now we must note that it is also the same as conversion. In all his references to conversion in the *Institutes* he treats it as if it were for him a subsidiary term

[1] *Institutes*, III, iii, 9.
[2] III, iii, 9.
[3] III, iii, 19.

Baptism and Conversion

equivalent to *poenitentia*. "Under the term *poenitentia*," he writes, "is comprehended the whole of conversion to God. . . . The term is derived in Hebrew from conversion or return, and in Greek from a change of mind and purpose."[4] It would seem to follow that infants are converted as well as regenerated at baptism, and that Calvin does not think of conversion as a distinctively later stage. But here again we are in sight of the fact that, while Luther, in speaking of baptismal regeneration, has in mind mainly infant baptism, Calvin (though holding equally to infant baptism) *thinks out* his doctrine rather in terms of adults.

Coming now to such a later Calvinist document as the Westminster Confession, we note again that conversion is far from being one of the key terms with which it operates. It occurs only in the section on Free Will, where it is said that the natural man is not able to convert himself, and where the juxtaposition occurs, "When God converts a sinner, and translates him into a state of grace." We may then ask what is expected by the Westminster standards of those who have been baptized in infancy, after they have grown up to years of understanding? The answer according to the Larger Catechism is that they are expected to *improve their baptism*. Question 167 asks, "How is our baptism to be improved by us?" And the answer is given finely as follows:

[4] III, iii, 5; cf. II, iii, 8.

The Christian Churches about Conversion

> The needful but much neglected duty of improving our baptism is to be performed by us all our life long, especially in time of temptation, and when we are present at the administration of it to others; by serious and thankful consideration of the nature of it, and of the ends for which Christ instituted it, the privileges and benefits conferred and sealed thereby, and our solemn vows made therein; by being humbled for our sinful defilement, our falling short of, and walking contrary to, the grace of baptism, and our engagements; by growing up to assurance of pardon of sin, and of all the blessings sealed to us in that sacrament; by drawing strength from the death and resurrection of Christ, into whom we are baptized, for the mortifying of sin, and quickening of grace; and by endeavouring to live by faith, to have our conversation in holiness and righteousness, as those that have therein given up their names to Christ; and to walk in brotherly love, as being baptized by the same Spirit into one body.

This conception of "improving our baptism," of making the remembrance of it determinative throughout the whole of later life, is true and original Reformation teaching, both Lutheran and Calvinist. I count it as a serious loss and defect that less has been made of it within the Reformed Churches in more recent times. One cause of this is that, when Calvinism came to be influenced by the later evangelical movements, which in so many ways

Baptism and Conversion

brought it great gain, this emphasis on baptism tended to give way to certain other emphases.

But let us ask more pointedly: Do the Westminster standards speak of any single critical turning point, such as later evangelicals mean by conversion, after years of discretion are reached? Such a crisis is of course certainly demanded in all who have *not* been regenerated (and converted) in infancy. What took place in others in infancy must now take place in them, if they are to be saved. But if we were right in suspecting that the standards were to be interpreted as meaning that only those are regenerated in infancy who, being of the number of the elect, either are destined to die in infancy or grow up as mental defectives, then it would follow that a crisis of regeneration is demanded of all others who are to be saved, after years of discretion. The standard term employed for this crisis is "effectual calling," which is therefore virtually equivalent, as regards its incidence, to regeneration; so that those who have not been so called are frequently referred to as "the unregenerate," and we have the phrase, "they who are effectually called and regenerated." [5] It is stated that all the elect are sooner or later effectually called. "All those whom God hath predestinated unto life, and those only, he is pleased, in his appointed and accepted time, effectually to call"—some in infancy but others in adult life. Here, as in Calvin himself, the doctrine of election governs everything. In dis-

[5] Chapter XIII, 1.

The Christian Churches about Conversion

cussing effectual calling in the *Institutes* Calvin writes that "God, for the purpose of displaying His own glory, withholds the efficacy of His Spirit from those whom He has not elected"; [6] and warns against the error of making man a co-operator with God, so that man's decision (*suffragium*) is required to ratify God's election of him. "It is false to say that election is essential only after we have embraced the gospel, and that from this it derives its validity." [7]

Two further points may be mentioned. Whereas, as we have seen, Calvin himself teaches along with the Lutheran formularies that regeneration only begins in baptism and is not then completed, there is only one place in the Westminster Confession where something like this is implied, namely, the phrase in Chapter XIII "the regenerate part (of believers)." This is significant in view of the fact that, according to Heppe's digest of the views of later Calvinist theologians, the usual teaching was that (as he quotes from one such theologian) "All regeneration is consummated in a single moment," or (as he quotes from another) "Regeneration is always instantaneous, or happens in an instant." [8] Secondly, we may note that whereas the Lutheran standards teach in opposition to the Roman view that all believers can and should have complete assurance of salvation, what the Westminster Confession

[6] Book III, xxiv, 2.
[7] Book III, xxiv, 3.
[8] English translation, p. 519.

Baptism and Conversion

says is that, while believers "may in this life be certainly assured that they are in a state of grace," and sure of it with "an infallible assurance," yet "This infallible assurance doth not so belong to the essence of faith, but that a true believer may wait long . . . before he be a partaker of it," though "it is the duty of all to seek it." [9]

[9] Chapter XVIII.

16

The Influence of the
Later Evangelical Movements

FINALLY, I pass from the Churches founded at the Reformation to the later evangelical movements. As was clearly indicated in Bishop Neill's statement which I began by quoting, it is to these movements that we owe the definitive use of the term conversion to denote a single critical experience in which an individual becomes a Christian after years of discretion are reached.

The earliest of these evangelical movements was German pietism. Spener himself (1635–1705), who is so often spoken of as "the father of pietism," did not indeed speak of conversion in quite this way. True to his Lutheran background, he continued to believe that regeneration takes place at baptism in infancy; but what is significant is that he insisted also on the necessity for true Christians of a second regeneration, and it is this latter that came to be spoken of among the pietists as conversion. It might be said, then, that the pietists set up afresh something of a double standard among Christians, however differently this was conceived from the double standard of the Romans. Once again, but this time as meaning those who

Baptism and Conversion

shared the experience of this second regeneration or conscious conversion, true Christians were distinguished from the ordinary run of Church members. Further, Spener taught that even after the second regeneration, a man may lapse again and yet again from the state of grace, so requiring further conversions—a position which we may contrast with the Calvinist teaching that a man once justified "can never fall from the state of justification." [1]

The Wesleyan movement in England was, of course, largely influenced by German pietism, but Wesley altogether dissociated regeneration from baptism, being the first clearly so to do. Unlike the Anabaptists, he held to baptism in infancy, yet would not at all allow that infants could be regenerated. Regeneration for him must be a conscious experience. But he followed the pietists in teaching that a regenerate person may lapse from his converted state, and may therefore experience more than one conversion. Actually Wesley himself did not make much use of the term conversion, though his followers soon came to make it a key term. It is really in his doctrine of assurance that the essence of Wesley's teaching is contained.[2] I would remind you again that Luther held, in opposition to the Roman teaching, that every Christian

---

[1] Westminster Confession, Chapter XI, 5.

[2] "The fundamental contribution of Methodism to the life and thought of the Church is the doctrine of Assurance"—H. B. Workman, *New History of Methodism*, Vol. I, p. 19; as quoted in *The Encyclopaedia of Religion and Ethics:* article on "Certainty," Vol. 3.

The Christian Churches about Conversion

must have complete assurance of salvation, nowise doubting the efficacy of God's baptismal grace; while Calvinism took an intermediate position between Rome and Luther, teaching the eminent *desirability* of the *certitudo salutis*. It was often attainable, the Calvinists said, but not essential, being a variable fruit of regeneration, and also manywise subject to illusion. To the Calvinist everything depends upon our *election*. We shall be regenerate if we have been elected; but the sure *knowledge* that we are elected and consequently regenerated, though highly desirable, does not necessarily follow.

But to the leaders of the evangelical movements the subjective consciousness is vital. There must be an experience—an experience of assured conversion which becomes the central thing in religion and, in Bishop Neill's words, "the beginning of the Christian life." A man is not a Christian until he has passed through this experience. To the question "Are you saved?" the answer "I do not know" was no longer accepted, just as Luther would not have accepted it—and here the Lutheran background of the earliest evangelicalism comes out clearly. Yet Luther's emphasis was not on an experience but on reliance on God's baptismal promise, while the evangelicals emphasized the conscious experience and therefore came to hold, as against Luther, that babies cannot be regenerated.

The evangelical movements were undoubtedly one source of the Romantic Movement, which stood also for a new emphasis on subjective experience. Schleiermacher,

Baptism and Conversion

the greatest of the Romantic theologians, defines theology as "a systematisation of the religious self-consciousness"; but where he thus uses the term self-consciousness, his successors preferred to speak of "religious experience." Hence derives the modern theological emphasis on religious experience, against which Karl Barth and his followers have so strongly reacted.

There can be no doubt of the very far-reaching influence exercised upon Protestant piety by these evangelical movements—even when what were regarded as the errors of pietism and evangelicalism were deliberately repudiated. I was myself brought up in the very rigorous Calvinism of the Scottish Highlands at the turn of the present century, and I shall conclude my historical sketch by trying to indicate in a very few words how far the Calvinist piety with which I was surrounded in these years was influenced by this later evangelicalism.

The doctrine of election still dominated everything. Whether or not we were regenerate was believed to depend on whether we had been elected. Further, we were still taught that assurance is not necessary to salvation, being in itself no part of saving faith, but a variable fruit of it. Our Confession had taught that "it is the duty of every one to seek it," but I think we were encouraged to give greater weight to it than the Confession alone would indicate, and I put that down very largely to the influence of the later evangelicalism—though something has also to be accredited to the direction taken by British Puri-

The Christian Churches about Conversion

tanism as over against Continental Calvinism. We were, I think, encouraged to be more introspective than was original Calvinism. Nor did we hear much about baptismal regeneration. Hardly were we taught to rely upon our baptism. The emphasis was upon our continued and confirmed and now fully deliberate commitment to Christ, as we grew up. Before we were admitted to communion, it was inquired of us whether we had so committed ourselves. On the other hand, a single, datable and conscious "experience of conversion" was not demanded, though many had an experience of this sort, and such experiences were hailed by all with joy and gratitude. But others grew up "in the nurture and admonition of the Lord" without being aware of any later crisis; and this, I think, was accepted with equal joy and gratitude. On the whole the typical methods of evangelistic "revivalism" were looked at askance. The religion of the Scottish Highlands in my childhood was thus, as it seems to me, a rigorous and traditional Calvinism affected in no negligible degree by later evangelicalism.

What I have so far tried to do, then, has been to explain the historical origins and later history of the divergence between the two views described in Bishop Neill's statement.

IV

THE NATURE OF THE CONVERSION EXPERIENCE

17

"Evangelical" Conversion Analyzed

HAVING now the historical facts before us, we have finally to enquire more closely into the nature and theological standing of that conversion experience which has been given the central place in what Bishop Neill called "the evangelical Free Churches and the evangelical movements within the more traditional Churches." Such experience of conversion is conceived as a conscious crisis, occurring no less in the hearts and minds of those who have been brought up "in the nurture and admonition of the Lord" than in those who now come to the Christian religion from another faith, and marking a reversal of direction after years of discretion have been reached. William James in his *Varieties of Religious Experience* defines conversion in this sense as "the process, gradual or sudden, by which a self, hitherto divided, and consciously wrong, inferior and unhappy, becomes unified and consciously right, superior and happy, in consequence of its firmer hold upon religious realities."[1] These are carefully chosen words, and I think that in a general way they would be accepted as a true definition.

[1] *Op. cit.*, p. 189.

Baptism and Conversion

James says "gradual or sudden," but this needs clarification. According to traditional teaching, both "catholic" and "evangelical," every man is at any given moment either in a state of sin or in a state of grace, and from this it follows that the transition from the one state to the other must accomplish itself in a single moment. But just as the catholic-minded identify this transition with regeneration at baptism, the evangelically-minded identify it with the later experience of conversion. Hence the conversion of which they speak *must* take place in a single indivisible moment. Thus when the evangelicals allow, as they commonly do, that some conversions are sudden but others gradual, they can only have in mind (if at the same time they hold to the orthodox view that there is no intermediate condition between the state of sin and the state of grace) the difference between a change which takes place without previous events leading up to it and a change which follows on a long period of inward struggle but which nevertheless, when it comes, happens equally in a single instant. James fully realizes this, and writes as follows:

> That the conversion should be instantaneous seems called for on this view, and the Moravian Protestants appear to have been the first to see this logical consequence. The Methodists soon followed suit, practically if not dogmatically, and a short time ere his death John Wesley wrote:—
> 'In London alone I found 652 members of our

The Nature of Conversion Experience

> Society who were exceeding clear in their experience, and whose testimony I found no reason to doubt. And every one of these (without a single exception) has declared that his deliverance from sin was instantaneous; that the change was wrought in a moment. Had half of these, or one third, or even one in twenty, declared it was *gradually* wrought in them, I should have believed this with regard to *them*, and thought that *some* were gradually sanctified and some instantaneously. But as I have not found, in so long a space of time, a single person speaking thus, I cannot but believe that sanctification is commonly, if not always, an instantaneous work.' [2]

James is right in saying that Wesley here makes his point "practically" rather than "dogmatically," yet in logic, and on the ground of his general theological beliefs, he ought to have made it dogmatically. On his premises conversion, as the transition from a state of sin to a state of grace, *must* be instantaneous, even if the subject himself could not point to the moment in which it took place.

There is of course no doubt at all of the reality and frequency of such conversion experiences, and there is as little doubt of their quite critical significance in the lives of those to whom they are given. Where different views emerge is rather in the interpretation of the experience, and most especially in the status and position accorded

[2] *Op. cit.*, p. 227. James's reference for the quotation from Wesley is Tyerman's *Life of Wesley*, I., p. 463.

Baptism and Conversion

to it within the whole sequence of the Christian life. Yet we must also be prepared to allow that the experience itself is partly determined by the interpretation, that is, by the expectations deriving from the doctrine which has been implanted in the minds of those undergoing it concerning the proper sequence of spiritual experience. Thus it is not only the interpretations of the experience, but also the experience itself, which will be different within the different traditions. Just as a conversion within Buddhism will not be exactly similar even on its purely psychological side to a conversion within a Christian context, so will a conversion within a Roman Catholic context not be psychologically identical with a conversion within a context of Methodist teaching. This fact must, however, be balanced against the other fact that we have here to do with an experience which in its most general features is common to the various traditions, being prior to the differing dogmatic interpretations that are put upon it.

As to these interpretations, the divergence with which we are here principally concerned is of course that between the two traditions that are now so often distinguished as the catholic-minded and the evangelically-minded; though, if we accept this nomenclature for our present purpose, we must not allow ourselves to be misled by it. According to Bishop Neill the evangelically-minded regard the conversion experience as "the beginning of real Christian life," and tend to hold that "no one is, or should be called a Christian" until this event has overtaken him,

The Nature of Conversion Experience

"Christian nurture, education and worship" in earlier years being no more than a "preparation" for this. This means that those who have been born into Christian families, who have been brought up "in the nurture and admonition of the Lord," and have exhibited as they grew up such devoutness and piety as very young children can exhibit, must nevertheless, before they can be called Christians, pass through a crisis of conversion at a later age.

What then are we to say about this? We may first ask whether it is in fact true that all who in later life were most worthy to be called Christians have passed through such an experience. It is difficult to believe that this is the case; and if it is not the case, then it cannot be held that such an experience is the criterion of men's spiritual status. When examples are called for, those that most readily spring to mind—and most of those studied by William James—are of individuals who have so far left the straight paths of their upbringing as to have had their lives set in a wrong direction; and it may be said that only in such cases is the conversion crisis exhibited in all its typical features. In such a case a man is converted in the most literal sense of turning right round, so that he now faces in the contrary direction. On the other hand it is true that even among those who may be said, in spite of lapses and failures such as Christians never cease to be subject to, to have grown up facing in the *right* direction through all their Christian upbringing, there is

Baptism and Conversion

very commonly a well-marked experience of a critical kind leading to greater consecration and more complete commitment. This is equally recognized by all Christian traditions and communions, but the different traditions interpret it differently. The more catholic traditions do not think of it as marking the beginning of the Christian life, but rather as a further stage in its development. They would speak first of the solemn experience which should accompany confirmation, when those who are already members of Christ's Body are further confirmed in the faith. But many, including the Roman Church, would think also of a *conversio a saeculo*, a call to follow the evangelical counsels and live the so-called "religious" life; a conversion indeed, but a conversion from the ordinary or secular Christian life to a higher way.

18

Psychological "Readjustment"

LET US, however, before proceeding further, enquire a little more closely into the nature of the conversion experience, having in mind particularly what the evangelically-minded would regard as typical cases. It has sometimes been doubted whether in its essential features it is a specifically *religious* experience at all. It is really, so it is said, a psychological readjustment, the reintegration of a personality that has been at odds with itself. There is of course no doubting that it is often closely associated with, and accompanied by, certain religious beliefs, but it is said that this is not always or necessarily so. It is claimed that the required experience of release can be achieved also by "depth-psychology" without any religious ideas or emotions being called into play at all; and there are those who hold that it is *better* achieved in this way. It is said, further, that the so-called "life-changing" practised by certain Christian groups is in reality more dependent upon psychological techniques than upon the appeal of the specifically Christian message. Also, there is no doubt that such conversion is usually associated with the age of puberty or adolescence. According to the statistical

Baptism and Conversion

tables printed in Starbuck's *Psychology of Religion* more than half a century ago, the greatest frequency is in the seventeenth year, and after the age of forty it is comparatively rare, psychological readjustment being very difficult to accomplish after that age. This fact is obviously patient of different interpretations, but the conclusion some draw from it is that the age of puberty will usually be accompanied by a deep emotional upheaval, and that such upheaval has no essential or invariable connection with the Christian or any other religion. I have heard Roman Catholics allow this to be true, and claim that it is better to have children confirmed in the faith, and brought to first communion, *before* this experience comes to them, so that they can, so to say, take it in their Christian stride, and face its rigours as fully committed Christians.

What are we ourselves to say to all this? Not a little of it we must, I think, allow to be true. But there are some considerations I would like to press very strongly.

First, I would say that such an experience is always at least a *moral* experience. It is a matter of psychology—yes, but of *moral* psychology. *Conscience* is always involved in it. There may indeed be psychopathic conditions in which no moral element is involved, where there is no uneasy conscience or cause for an uneasy conscience, but these do not involve any experience such as would be associated with the word conversion.

I would, however, go further. I am convinced that such

The Nature of Conversion Experience

an experience of conversion is always more than merely moral. The conflict which it involves is not only a conflict between better and worse, between the lesser and the greater good, but is always rooted in a deep-lying sense of frustration, and indeed of sin, such as betokens a reference to ultimate and transcendent reality, and to what Tillich has taught us to call "our ultimate concern." There is indeed, as he would say, an "ontological" reference in it. William James is quite clear about this. In the definition I quoted from him he says that in conversion the divided self "becomes unified . . . *in consequence of its firmer hold upon religious realities.*" Even of conversion experiences outside the Christian context this is true. Even the Stoic philosophers, in making so much of conversion, related it in this way to transcendent reality. The sense of "the Whole (*to holon*)," they said, was always involved in it.

19

The Relation of such Readjustment to the Christian Gospel

THIS, however, leads us to ask, What is the relation between that experience of psychological readjustment which is conversion and the Christian gospel? In attempting to answer this question, we must indeed keep it in mind that there are Jews, Buddhists and Mohammedans who have had overwhelming experiences of this kind, who have obtained inward peace through them, who have "come to themselves" as the Prodigal Son came to himself, who have come to terms with their own consciences in the sight of God or of such gods as they knew and in the light of such truths as had been revealed to them —and that with a completeness of self-commitment and self-surrender such as would put to shame many of ourselves who call ourselves Christians. William James's type of "twice-born man" is often to be found in India and in Islamic lands.

We are thus led to ask, adapting the Pauline phrase, "What advantage then hath the Christian?" I would reply, again in St. Paul's words, "Much every way." But chiefly I would make two points.

The Nature of Conversion Experience

First, I would affirm that the Christian gospel is such as to impart to the moral alternative a more decisive character and a greater solemnity than it ever had before. When our Lord came preaching that the time was fulfilled, when He summoned men to repentance because the Kingdom of God was at hand, not only was the issue made clearer, and the lists more cleanly drawn than they had hitherto been, but the urgency of swift and immediate decision was brought home to men in a more compelling way. I believe the Christian gospel has been successful in bringing about in men that moral-psychological readjustment of which we have been speaking, as was no previous teaching or preaching. Mohammedanism, it must be remembered, is a post-Christian type of spirituality; and certain of those movements within modern Hinduism which approach nearest to the evangelical pattern have not been uninfluenced by Christianity. In our own homelands also, I know some men who are "twice-born" in James's sense if any men are, men of a broken and contrite heart, and yet who do not profess the Christian faith —"converted" men, if you like, in the second of the two senses of that word which I have distinguished; but I am equally sure that they could not be what they are, or have experienced what they have experienced, if they had not the Christian tradition behind them. It was said, for instance, of the Cambridge philosopher Henry Sidgwick that he manifested every Christian virtue except faith; and Lord David Cecil has more recently been so

Baptism and Conversion

bold as to characterise the unbelieving Thomas Hardy as "one of the most Christian spirits that ever lived."

The preaching of the Christian gospel, then, placed all those who heard it in a more solemn crisis of decision than they had ever before encountered. Yet—and this is my second point—it is of the very first importance to note that this was not only because they were made to realize with a new clarity the critical nature of the situation in which men had always stood before God. It was also because they were now confronted with a new spiritual situation. It was not merely that the Christian way of putting the case was more effective in persuading men to face up to it, but that there was now a new case to put to them. "After John the Baptist was put in prison, Jesus came into Galilee, preaching the gospel of God, and saying, The time is fulfilled, and the kingdom of God is at hand; change your minds and believe this good news." [1] The point is that it was really news. The time of which our Lord spoke (*kairos*) had not always been there. But now men were placed in a new situation and before a new decision. A whole new economy of things, a new dispensation, was opening out before them. A new age was dawning, a new era in the world's history that would afterwards come to be marked even by a new system of dating—so that everything would now be regarded as being either B.C. or A.D., as we say. And the decision men were required to make was whether they would enter

[1] Mark i, 14–15.

The Nature of Conversion Experience

into the heritage of this new era or shut themselves out from it by remaining as it were within the old era—"still under the law," as St. Paul afterwards put it. It is for this reason that, despite all that may be said of conversional readjustments within other faiths, such experiences within Christianity have, even on the psychological level, a character that is elsewhere rare. The new situation was such as to demand a more radical readjustment, which therefore gave rise to a completer and more satisfying experience of psychological release than had hitherto been likely to supervene. But what Christ demanded was not just an experience of conversion; He desired that men should be converted to the specifically Christian outlook, that is, to an outlook determined throughout by the new situation which had been created by His advent.

20

Is a "Conversion Experience" Necessary?

IT IS this distinction which I wish finally to develop, and I think the best way of doing so is to return to the question posed to us at the outset in the quotation from Bishop Neill. Should we expect or demand, in the case of those who have been brought up from infancy within the Christian faith and fellowship and "in the nurture and admonition of the Lord," a single decisive experience of readjustment such as can be called conversion? We must now try to answer that question as clearly as we can.

We shall all agree that nobody should or can be called a Christian until he has been adjusted to the new situation brought about by the coming of God to man in the flesh and by the preaching of the Christian gospel. On this all parties think alike. The disagreement is only between those who hold that in the case of those brought up within the Christian Church this adjustment should normally be, in Bishop Neill's words, "a continuous process," gradually accomplishing itself as the child grows into adolescence and manhood (and then the man into maturer age); and those who affirm, again in Bishop Neill's words, that "no one is, or should be called, a Christian,"

The Nature of Conversion Experience

or has made a "beginning of real Christian life," until a crisis of readjustment has been experienced by him in adolescence or maturity.

Already, when discussing baptism, I so far ventured a judgement concerning this question as to say that in my view, and in the broadest sense, real Christian life begins when an infant is received by baptism into the Christian community. Such an infant, I said, is already a Christian infant—the only kind of Christian that God desires him to be at that age and stage. I would now say further that the desirable and proper course of events is that the seed of Christian life thus sown should mature steadily and gradually into Christian adolescence and manhood or womanhood. It is expected of every Christian child that, as he grows up, he should more and more become confirmed in the faith, sealing by his own deliberate decision the commitment which was made for him in his infancy. Very often the transition from the Christian outlook of childhood to the deliberate Christian commitment of later years will not come merely by way of slow and imperceptible gradations, but will be marked by a single, well-defined and datable crisis of experience, a more or less sudden awakening to the issues involved in Christian commitment, and the taking of a single firm and solemn decision. It is entirely natural that such an experience should most commonly supervene at the age of puberty, the age which marks the mental as well as the emotional and physiological transition from childhood to

Baptism and Conversion

maturity. On the other hand, there are as many whose passage from the simple Christian outlook of childhood to the personally confirmed Christianity of later years is marked by no such single outstanding experience, but comes about by slow gradations.

I should therefore very much deprecate any teaching which makes everything hinge upon a single conversional readjustment, so as to demand or encourage it in every case. Such teaching has had several unfortunate consequences. It not infrequently leads to a quite insalutary mental distress in those whose own Christian experience, though equally authentic, has not followed this pattern. Also it makes others, who have experienced such a conversion, place what I can only call *too much* reliance upon it, encouraging them to think that no further growth or reformation is necessary. They are too much "at ease in Zion." Nor must we forget that there are many Christians, including some of the greatest saints, who would have to say that, if they have had one conversion, they have had more than one. I remember how Dr. Alexander Whyte used to quote from one of his beloved Puritans the saying, "The Christian life is made up of ever new beginnings."

I should put it this way. What is important is not that men should have passed through a particular sort of experience but that, whatever their experiences, they should now be true Christians. There was nothing that our Lord more emphatically said than that men are to be known

The Nature of Conversion Experience

by the fruit they bear. He did not say, He could not say that men are *saved* by their fruits—that would be "salvation by works"; but He said they were to be *known* by their fruits. "A good tree cannot bring forth evil fruit, neither can a corrupt tree bring forth good fruit. . . . Wherefore by their fruits ye shall know them." [1] What is important, I say, is not that men should have passed through the sort of experience examples of which William James collects in his famous book. There is nothing exclusively Christian about such psychological readjustment and release, though for the reasons which I have already adduced it is altogether more common within the Christian tradition than anywhere else. What is important is what men are converted *to*. What is important is that, whether by gradual adjustment or sudden readjustment, men should in the end come to be adjusted to *the authentic and full Christian outlook*. And it is to be feared that many who look back on conversion experiences, perhaps in early youth, such as would have furnished William James with some of his most striking examples, are living with a pathetically narrow, and enfeebled and perverted Christian outlook, and are far from having entered into the full heritage of the "new age" which Christ came to announce, and of the freedom wherewith He sought to make men free. Is this perhaps true of ourselves? Is it true of myself? I shall never forget how once, when I had been preaching about conversion at a united Lenten

[1] Matthew vii, 18, 20.

Baptism and Conversion

service in an American city, one of the ministers present, for whose Christian wisdom I had and still have the greatest regard, startled me by saying, "The most obstructive and narrow-visioned people in my congregation are some of those who long ago had a dramatic conversion experience and have rested at ease in their own very parochial Zion ever since."

What I have been saying, then, is that what is to be expected of those who are received in infancy into the fold of the Christian fellowship, and who are brought up from earliest childhood within the discipline of that fellowship, is that they should grow up into the enjoyment of a mature and adult Christian faith and into the practice of a full Christian life; that what matters is not what "experiences" they should have passed through, but whether in the end they have come to have the mind of Christ; not (as I have ventured to put it badly for the sake of driving home the point) whether they are converted, but what they are converted to.

But—and it is an all-important "but"—the sad fact is that very many of those who have thus been received into the Christian fellowship in infancy, and very many also who after their reception have continued to receive Christian upbringing and instruction, have afterwards fallen away from the strait path of their upbringing. I do not mean merely that they have fallen into various sins. We all of us fall into various sins. I mean that they have

The Nature of Conversion Experience

ceased to feel themselves committed. They no longer put their trust in Christ for their salvation. They have spurned the pledge of their baptism. They have drifted away from the Christian fellowship. We have to face the fact that something like this is true of great multitudes in our day —men and women who were nevertheless baptized into Christ in their infancy and received Christian nurture in their tender years, and who perhaps for a time continued in the way of their upbringing. It is clear, then, that in such numerous cases nothing can serve but a new beginning, a new orientation, a radical change of direction. And that is the true evangelical sense of the word conversion—a "turning round again" to face the long-forsaken light, a return to the Lord after days or years of apostasy. Just as the prophets of Israel were always calling upon the apostate people to return unto the Lord, so the Christian evangelist must call upon the multitude of lapsed members of the Body of Christ to return to His fold.

I shall bring these lectures to a close, adding only a single concluding remark of my own, by quoting two passages from an address delivered by Alec Vidler during the Mission to Oxford University in the spring of 1938. The address was entitled "Do we need Conversion?" and it was published, together with the rest of the addresses delivered by him on the same occasion, under the title *God's Demand and Man's Response*.[2]

[2] London: Unicorn Press, 1938.

Baptism and Conversion

First, this:

> The revivalist movements, which have been, and are likely to remain, periodically recurring events in the history of Christianity, tend to bring the idea of conversion into discredit among wise and balanced minds by their aggressive insistence that all real Christians, as they would say, must undergo a psychological experience or change, sudden in its incidence and uniform in its pattern. That the managers of revivalist movements should like to work according to a uniform and therefore easily manageable technique is intelligible but it is gravely deplorable. For the attempt to dragoon souls into conformity with a single, and in fact none too healthy, pattern of spiritual experience disregards the diverse means by which the Spirit of God actually works. A wise master of the spiritual life has said: 'We ought each to respect the pattern that God seeks to produce in us,' and in no two cases are we to suppose that the pattern will be precisely identical. Not the abstract uniformity of *law*, but the infinite and rich diversity of *personality* is the guiding clue to God's creative purpose.[3]

And then this:

> Christian conversion is a process, a life-long process. It is not a sudden event that can be fin-

[3] Pp. 77f.

The Nature of Conversion Experience

ished and done with. It is a gradual transformation of personality through the love of God in Christ. For many the process does begin with an apparently sudden realization of the claims and love of Christ; that is what is called "sudden" conversion. And the very fact that it is called "sudden" implies that it is not the only possible or even the normal manner of conversion. Undoubtedly for others, and perhaps for most, the initial experience, which we call conversion in the narrower sense, need not be sudden. It may be a realization that dawns slowly, and it may be met by a personal decision that is neither sudden nor dramatic, but is none the less deliberate and final. However it may be in your case, what I am saying now is that there must be, in one way or another this initial conversion, this decisive self-commitment. Consider it for yourself in this way: Can you say—not precisely *when* you were converted—but whether you are now a converted Christian in the sense of being one who has realized Christ's absolute claim upon your life and who acknowledges himself *bound* to Christ and the Christian way of life whatever be the cost? If you cannot say this yet, I trust this mission will assist you to make the definite response and self-commitment which Christ demands—or at least to see clearly what issues are at stake.[4]

Some things in what is there said I should perhaps put in a slightly different way, but with the general intent

[4] Pp. 81f.

Baptism and Conversion

of it I should cordially agree. And I should also cordially agree with some words written for one of our Church of Scotland publications by my friend the Rev. J. Fraser McLuskey:

> It is true that 'decisions' for Christ may be made in very different ways and that they must be made more than once. But however they are made, they must be made at least once. We don't fall up the spiritual stairs. We climb them one step at a time. And the steps are acts of conscious commitment of the whole self to the God we meet in Jesus Christ.

What is vital is that, by whatever steps and stages, and through whatever experiences, we should now be definitely committed; and that our commitment should be, not to an abridged understanding of what the Gospel portends, but to the whole fulness of Christ and the whole breadth of the new outlook on life with which He came to endow us.

INDEX

INDEX

A

Allier, 53
Amos, 60
Anabaptists, 84
Anglican Church, Anglicanism, 32–33, 43

Articles of Religion, 32, 33
Assurance, doctrine of, 84
Augsburg Confession, 24, 73
Augustine (St.), 63

B

Baptism in the New Testament (Cullmann), 20, 43n.
Baptist Churches, Baptists, 17, 38–40
Baptist Confession (1611), 38–39
Barth, Karl, 23, 24, 43, 86

Book of Common Order, 46
Book of Common Prayer, The, 32
Brunner, Emil, 23, 24
Buddhism, Buddhists, 57, 94, 100
Bultmann, Rudolf, 20, 23

C

Calvin, John, 27–31, 32, 34, 35, 42, 47, 77, 78, 80, 81
See also Calvinism
Calvinism, Calvinists, 24, 26, 27, 35, 36, 61, 74, 77, 79, 84, 85, 86, 87
See also Calvin, John
Cardiphonia (Newton), 72

Index

Catholic Encyclopaedia, The, 18, 19n., 68, 69n.
Catholicism
 See Roman Catholic Church
Cecil, Lord David, 101
Christian's Great Interest, The (Guthrie), 71
Church
 invisible, 34, 45
 membership, 15
 visible, 34, 45
 See also names of individual churches and movements
Church of Scotland, 37, 46, 112
Cicero, 56
Commentary on Galatians (Luther), 74
Confirmation, 15, 19, 20–21, 23, 67
Constantine, 68
Conversion (Paterson), 53
Conversion: Christian and Non-Christian (Underwood), 53
Conversion: from Alexander the Great to Augustine of Hippo (Nock), 53
Council of Trent
 Catechism of, 20
 Decrees of, 74
Covenant (O. T.), 58, 61
Crypto-Calvinism, 26
Cullmann, Oscar, 20, 23, 43

D

David, 60
Declaratory Acts (Scotland), 36–37
Deutero-Isaiah, 60
 See also Isaiah
Diary of Mrs. Kitty Trevelyan (Trevelyan), 72
Divine-Human Encounter, The (Brunner), 23
Doctrine of Baptism, The (Barth), 23
Driver, G. R., 60

E

Eastern Orthodox Church
 See Orthodox Church
Elect, Election, 33–37, 80–81, 86

Index

Eleusinian Mystery, 54
Encyclopaedia of Religion and Ethics, The, 24n., 25n., 70, 84n.
Evangelical movements, 73, 79, 80, 83–87, 91

Evangelism, Commission on (W. C. C.), 13
Ezekiel, 59, 60

F

First Helvetic Confession, 36
Formula of Concord, 24, 73–76

Free Churches, 15, 91

G

God's Demand and Man's Response (Vidler), 109

Guthrie, 71

H

Hardy, Thomas, 102
Heidegger, Martin, 35
Heiler, Friedrich, 75

Heppe, 35, 81
Hinduism, Hindus, 57, 101

I

Imitation of Christ, The (à Kempis), 72
Institutes (Calvin), 27, 29, 77, 81

Isaiah, 60, 61
   See also Deutero-Isaiah
Islam
   See Mohammedanism

Index

J

James, William, 57, 91, 92, 93, 95, 99, 100, 101, 107
Jeremiah, 60
Jew, Judaism, 22, 52, 61, 100
See also Piety, Hebrew
John (St.), 57
Justification (Marshall), 71

K

Kingdom of Christ, The (Maurice), 25n., 45
Koinonia, 44

L

La spiritualité chrétienne (Pourrat), 72
Law, William, 72
Letters (Rutherford), 72
Luther, Martin, 22–25, 27, 28, 30, 31, 34, 68, 70, 71, 72, 74, 75, 77, 78, 84–85
See also Lutheranism
Lutheranism, Lutherans, 22–25, 26, 27, 28, 30, 43, 70–76, 79, 81
See also Luther, Martin

M

Marshall, 71
Maurice, Frederick Denison, 25, 45, 46, 48
McLuskey, J. Fraser, 112
Medieval Church, 34, 67

Methodism, Methodists, 84n., 92, 94
See also Wesley, John; Wesleyan movement

Index

Mohammedanism, Mohammedans, 100, 101
See also Moslem

Moravians, 92
Moslem, 52
See also Mohammedanism

N

Neill, Bishop Stephen, 13–15, 41, 83, 85, 87, 91, 94, 104
New Testament, 16–17, 18, 20, 23, 41, 43

Newman, John Henry, 62, 68
Newton, John, 72
Nock, A. D., 53, 54–55

O

Old Testament, 58, 59, 60, 61, 63

Orphism, 55
Orthodox Church, 14, 20

P

Paedobaptism, Paedobaptists, 17, 28
Paterson, W. P., 53
Paul (St.), 17, 31, 63, 100, 103
Penance, Penitence, 20–21, 25, 28, 67, 73
Pietism, 73, 83–84, 86
Piety, Hebrew, 58

Post-Reformation Churches, 38, 39
Pourrat, 72
Pre-Reformation Church, 18, 67, 68
Protestantism
See specific denominations and movements

Index

Psychologie de la Conversion chez les peuples non-civilisés (Allier), 53

Psychology of Religion (Starbuck), 98
Puritanism, 71, 86–87

R

Reformation, 22, 33, 38, 70, 71, 79
 See also Reformed tradition; Reformers
Reformation Churches, 83
Reformed Churches, 33, 36, 79
Reformed Dogmatics (Heppe), 35
Reformed tradition, 28, 42, 44, 77–82
 See also Reformation; Reformers
Reformers, 22, 23, 33
 See also Calvin, John; Luther, Martin; Reformation; Reformed tradition; Zwinglianism
Revivalist movements, 110
Roman Catholic Church, 14, 18–21, 22, 28, 42, 61, 67, 68, 71, 75, 77, 94, 96, 98
 See also Romanism
Romanism, 23, 24–25, 27, 43, 57, 63, 68, 73, 75, 81, 84, 85
 See also Roman Catholic Church
Romantic Movement, 85
Rutherford, Samuel, 72

S

Salvation, 20, 24, 25, 26, 27, 38, 42, 76, 109
Samuel, 60
Saxon Visitation Articles, Saxon Visitors, 26–27, 30, 31, 36
Schleiermacher, Friedrich, 85
Serious Call to a Devout and Holy Life, A (Law), 72

Sidgwick, Henry, 101
Small Catechism (Luther), 22, 73
Smith, W. Robertson, 60
Spener, 83, 84
Starbuck, 98
State Churches (Europe), 14
Stoicism, 55–56, 99

Index

T

Theodore of Mopsuestia, 60
Theology of the New Testament (Bultmann), 20

Thirty-nine Articles
   See Articles of Religion
Thomas à Kempis, 72
Tillich, Paul, 99

U

Underwood, A. C., 53, 57

V

Varieties of Religious Experience, The (James), 57, 91

Vidler, Alec, 109

W

Wesley, John, 63, 64, 84, 92, 93
   See also Methodism; Wesleyan movement
Wesleyan movement, 84–85
   See also Methodism; Wesley, John

Westminster Confession, 33–35, 42, 78, 80, 81, 84n.
Westminster Larger Catechism, 34, 78
Whyte, Alexander, 106
World Council of Churches, 13

Z

Zwinglianism, 36

```
BT                    106201
790
.B3
1963    Baillie, John
            Baptism and conversion.
```

HIEBERT LIBRARY
Fresno Pacific College - M. B. Seminary
Fresno, Calif. 93702